CARRIE WILLIAMS CLIFFORD

AND

CARRIE LAW MORGAN FIGGS

WRITINGS OF
CARRIE WILLIAMS CLIFFORD AND
CARRIE LAW MORGAN FIGGS

AFRICAN-AMERICAN WOMEN WRITERS, 1910–1940

HENRY LOUIS GATES, JR. *GENERAL EDITOR*

Jennifer Burton *Associate Editor*

OTHER TITLES IN THIS SERIES

CARRIE WILLIAMS CLIFFORD

AND

CARRIE LAW MORGAN FIGGS

WRITINGS OF
CARRIE WILLIAMS CLIFFORD
AND
CARRIE LAW MORGAN FIGGS

Introduction by
P. JANE SPLAWN

G. K. HALL & CO.
An Imprint of Simon & Schuster Macmillan
New York

Prentice Hall International
London Mexico City New Delhi Singapore Sydney Toronto

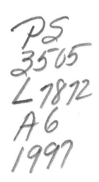

PS
3505
L7872
A6
1997

Introduction copyright © 1997 by P. Jane Splawn

G. K. Hall & Co.
An Imprint of Simon & Schuster Macmillan
1633 Broadway
New York, New York 10019

Library of Congress Catalog Card Number: 96-38729

Printed in the United States of America

Printing Number
1 2 3 4 5 6 7 8 9 10

Library of Congress Cataloging-in-Publication Data

Clifford, Carrie Williams, 1862–1934
    [Selections. 1996]
    Writings of Carrie Williams Clifford and Carrie Law Morgan Figgs / Carrie Williams Clifford, Carrie Law Morgan Figgs ; introduction by P. Jane Splawn.
        p. cm. — (African-American women writers, 1910–1940)
    Includes bibliographical references (p.).
    ISBN 0-7838-1435-6 (alk. paper)
    1. Afro-American women—Literary collections. 2. Afro-Americans—Literary collections. I. Figgs, Carrie Law Morgan. Selections. 1996. II. Title III. Series
PS3505.L7872A6 1996
810.8'09287'08996073—dc20   96-38729
                                                                CIP

This paper meets the requirements of ANSI/NISO Z39.48.1992 (Permanence of Paper).

C O N T E N T S

GENERAL EDITORS' PREFACE

The past decade of our literary history might be thought of as the era of African-American women writers. Culminating in the awarding of the Pulitzer Prize to Toni Morrison and Rita Dove and the Nobel Prize for Literature to Toni Morrison in 1993 and characterized by the presence of several writers—Toni Morrison, Alice Walker, Maya Angelou, and the Delaney Sisters, among others—on the *New York Times* Best Seller List, the shape of the most recent period in our literary history has been determined in large part by the writings of black women.

This, of course, has not always been the case. African-American women authors have been publishing their thoughts and feelings at least since 1773, when Phillis Wheatley published her book of poems in London, thereby bringing poetry directly to bear upon the philosophical discourse over the African's "place in nature" and his or her place in the great chain of being. The scores of words published by black women in America in the nineteenth century—most of which were published in extremely limited editions and never reprinted—have been republished in new critical editions in the forty-volume *Schomburg Library of Nineteenth-Century Black Women Writers*. The critical response to that series has led to requests from scholars and students alike for a similar series, one geared to the work by black women published between 1910 and the beginning of World War II.

African-American Women Writers, 1910–1940 is designed to bring back into print many writers who otherwise would be unknown to contemporary readers, and to increase the availability of lesser-known texts by established writers who originally published during this critical period in African-American letters. This series implicitly acts as a chronological sequel to the Schomburg series, which focused on the origins of the black female literary tradition in America.

In less than a decade, the study of African-American women's writings has grown from its promising beginnings into a firmly established field in departments of English, American Studies, and African-American Studies. A comparison of the form and function of the original series and this sequel illustrates this dramatic shift. The *Schomburg Library* was published at the cusp of focused academic investigation into the interplay between race and gender. It covered the extensive period from the publication of Phillis Wheatley's *Poems on Various Subjects, Religious and Moral* in 1773 through the "Black Women's Era" of 1890–1910, and was designed to be an inclusive series of the major early texts by black women writers. The Schomburg Library provided a historical backdrop for black women's writings of the 1970s and 1980s, including the works of writers such as Toni Morrison, Alice Walker, Maya Angelou, and Rita Dove.

African-American Women Writers, 1910–1940 continues our effort to provide a new generation of readers access to texts—historical, sociological, and literary—that have been largely "unread" for most of this century. The series bypasses works that are important both to the period and the tradition, but that are readily available, such as Zora Neale Hurston's *Their Eyes Were Watching God*, Jessie Fauset's *Plum Bun* and *There Is Confusion*, and Nella Larsen's *Quicksand* and *Passing*. Our goal is to provide access to a wide variety of rare texts. The series includes Fauset's two other novels, *The Chinaberry Tree: A Novel of American Life* and *Comedy: American Style*, and Hurston's short play *Color Struck*, since these are not yet widely available. It also features works by virtually unknown writers, such as *A Tiny Spark*, Christina Moody's slim volume of poetry self-published in 1910, and *Reminiscences of School Life, and Hints on Teaching*, written by Fanny Jackson Coppin in the last year of her life (1913), a multi-genre work combining an autobiographical sketch and reflections on trips to England and South Africa, complete with pedagogical advice.

Cultural Studies' investment in diverse resources allows the historic scope of the *African-American Women Writers* series to be more focused than the *Schomburg Library* series, which covered works written over a 137-year period. With few exceptions, the authors included in the *African-American Women Writers* series wrote their major works between 1910 and 1940. The texts reprinted include all the works by each particular author that are not otherwise readily obtainable. As a result, two volumes contain works originally published after 1940. The Charlotte Hawkins Brown volume includes her book of etiquette published in 1941, *The Correct Thing To Do—To Say—To Wear*. One of the poetry volumes contains Maggie Pogue Johnson's *Fallen Blossoms*, published in 1951, a compilation of all her previously published and unpublished poems.

Excavational work by scholars during the past decade has been crucial to the development of *African-American Women Writers, 1910–1940*. Germinal bibliographical sources such as Ann Allen Shockley's *Afro-American Women Writers 1746–1933* and Maryemma Graham's *Database of African-American Women Writers* made the initial identification of texts possible. Other works were brought to our attention by scholars who wrote letters sharing their research. Additional texts by selected authors were then added, so that many volumes contain the complete oeuvres of particular writers. Pieces by authors without enough published work to fill an entire volume were grouped with other pieces by genre.

The two types of collections, those organized by author and those organized by genre, bring out different characteristics of black women's writings of the period. The collected works of the literary writers illustrate that many of them were experimenting with a variety of forms. Mercedes Gilbert's volume, for example, contains her 1931 collection *Selected Gems of Poetry, Comedy, and Drama, Etc.*, as well as her 1938 novel *Aunt Sarah's Wooden God*. Georgia Douglas Johnson's volume contains her plays and short stories in addition to her poetry. Sarah Lee Brown Fleming's volume combines her 1918 novel *Hope's Highway* with her 1920 collection of poetry, *Clouds and Sunshine*.

The generic volumes both bring out the formal and thematic similarities among many of the writings and highlight the striking individuality of particular writers. Most of the plays in the volume of one-acts are social dramas whose tragic endings can be clearly attributed to miscegenation and racism. Within the context of these other plays, Marita Bonner's expressionistic theatrical vision becomes all the more striking.

The volumes of *African-American Women Writers, 1910–1940* contain reproductions of more than one hundred previously published texts, including twenty-nine plays, seventeen poetry collections, twelve novels, six autobiographies, five collections of short biographical sketches, three biographies, three histories of organizations, three black histories, two anthologies, two sociological studies, a diary, and a book of etiquette. Each volume features an introduction by a contemporary scholar that provides crucial biographical data on each author and the historical and critical context of her work. In some cases, little information on the authors was available outside of the fragments of biographical data contained in the original introduction or in the text itself. In these instances, editors have documented the libraries and research centers where they tried to find information, in the hope that subsequent scholars will continue the necessary search to find the "lost" clues to the women's stories in the rich stores of papers, letters, photographs, and other primary materials scattered throughout the country that have yet to be fully catalogued.

Many of the thrilling moments that occurred during the development of this series were the result of previously fragmented pieces of these women's histories suddenly coming together, such as Adele Alexander's uncovering of an old family photograph picturing her own aunt with Addie Hunton, the author Alexander was researching. Claudia Tate's examination of Georgia Douglas Johnson's papers in the Moorland-Spingarn Research Center of Howard University resulted in the discovery of a wealth of previously unpublished work.

The slippery quality of race itself emerged during the construction of the series. One of the short novels originally intended for inclusion in the series had to be cut when the family of the author protested that the writer was not of African descent. Another case involved Louise Kennedy's sociological study *The Negro Peasant Turns Inward*. The fact that none of the available biographical material on Kennedy specifically mentioned race, combined with some coded criticism in a review in the *Crisis*, convinced editor Sheila Smith McKoy that Kennedy was probably white.

These women, taken together, began to chart the true vitality, and complexity, of the literary tradition that African-American women have generated, using a wide variety of forms. They testify to the fact that the monumental works of Hurston, Larsen, and Fauset, for example, emerged out of a larger cultural context; they were not exceptions or aberrations. Indeed, their contributions to American literature and culture, as this series makes clear, were fundamental not only to the shaping of the African-American tradition but to the American tradition as well.

Henry Louis Gates, Jr.
Jennifer Burton

PUBLISHER'S NOTE

In the *African-American Women Writers, 1910–1940* series, G. K. Hall not only is making available previously neglected works that in many cases have been long out of print, we are also, whenever possible, publishing these works in facsimiles reprinted from their original editions including, when available, reproductions of original title pages, copyright pages, and photographs.

When it was not possible for us to reproduce a complete facsimile edition of a particular work (for example, if the original exists only as a handwritten draft or is too fragile to be reproduced), we have attempted to preserve the essence of the original by resetting the work exactly as it originally appeared. Therefore, any typographical errors, strikeouts, or other anomalies reflect our efforts to give the reader a true sense of the original work.

We trust that these facsimile and reprint editions, together with the new introductory essays, will be both useful and historically enlightening to scholars and students alike.

INTRODUCTION

BY P. JANE SPLAWN[1]

"Lifting as we climb," the late nineteenth-century motto of the black women's era, underscores key issues of duty, racial uplift, service, and, implicitly, values of teaching for black women. Adapting the cult of true womanhood to their own purposes,[2] black women lent their voices to both the church and the community. Many black women felt that they were able to reach a larger, more diverse black audience through their creative writings. At times these writers would appeal to black women's religious joy or to what Jacqueline Grant insightfully labels "Black women's Jesus."[3] Two such writers from the pre–Harlem Renaissance era are Carrie Williams Clifford and Carrie Law Morgan Figgs, black teachers and community leaders who used poetry and drama to effect social change.

Black women teachers were frequently called upon to lead their communities in matters of social protest as well as to provide models of social decorum. In her discussion of black women teachers of the South, Cynthia Neverton-Morton points out that "[w]hile it would have been easier for the women to see only the obstacles to quality education, they chose instead to concentrate on such positive factors as community involvement, community betterment, and enriching the lives of thousands of black children."[4] Recognizing that they could reach a larger portion of the black community through creative writing, these black women teachers often used poetry, drama, and fiction to promote community uplift. Writers such as Mary Burrill, a black educator at Dunbar High School in Washington, D.C., chose the medium of drama to underscore the immense need for birth control information for blacks, especially poor blacks. Other black women teachers used creative writing to address social injustice: Alice Dunbar-Nelson takes on the issue of black patriotism in racist America in her play *Mine Eyes Have Seen*, and poet-playwright Georgia Douglas Johnson lambasts the savagery of lynching in the play *A Sunday Morning in the South*.

Like their contemporaries Burrill, Dunbar-Nelson, and Johnson, Carrie Williams Clifford and Carrie Law Morgan Figgs wrote poetry and plays for the "betterment" of the race. Clifford avers in the "Preface" to *Race Rhymes* that she has selected the genre of poetry to present "serious" racial and gender concerns because "this may often be done more impressively through rhyme than in elegant prose dissertation."[5] Similarly, Figgs states in her "Introduction" to *Poetic Pearls* that the impetus to publish her poetry stems from her "hav[ing] given several years of service in the class room as a teacher and several years as Grand Most Ancient Matron of Heroines of Jericho," an organization comprised of the wives of black Masons. Just as black female jazz, blues, and gospel artists used their music to reach wider audiences (in taverns as well as in churches, school auditoriums, etc.), black women such as Clifford and Figgs used their poetry and plays to communicate with the entire black community.

Carrie Williams Clifford (1862–1934) was born just one year before Abraham Lincoln signed the Emancipation Proclamation, while the United States was in the midst of the Civil War. Though she herself was born free in Chillicothe, Ohio, many of her fellow African Americans were still enslaved.[6] Some of the details of Clifford's life are significant[7]: she was born into a middle-class family—her mother[8] ran a successful business in Columbus, Ohio, the city where Clifford received her education and where she would later found the Ohio Federation of Colored Women's Clubs, one of the first organizations of its kind in the country. Clifford's childhood roots in Ohio, a state famous for its strong abolitionist sentiments, seemed to instill in her a sense that she could indeed make her mark on the world. Cleveland, where she lived for most of her tenure in Ohio, was a fairly relaxed, liberal city during the second half of the nineteenth century. Clifford seemed to agree that Cleveland was more progressive racially than most places.[9] In her 1908 article "Cleveland and Its Colored People," she makes plain the link between less race prejudice and individual achievement. Clifford avers that "[t]he surprising progress made by our people in Cleveland is due to the slight amount of prejudice encountered by them here, and is an indication of what, with a full, free and unlimited opportunity, the colored people could become."[10]

Clifford left Ohio to teach school for a time in Parkersburg, West Virginia, before her marriage in 1886 to William H. Clifford, a lawyer and Republican member of the Ohio State Legislature. The couple had two sons, and in 1908 the family moved to Washington, D.C., where Clifford combined an active political life, working with the NAACP and other activist organizations, with a rigorous intellectual existence. Owing in part to her close proximity to Howard University, visitors to her home included such intellectuals and literary artists as Mary Church Terrell, Alain Locke, Georgia Douglas Johnson, and W. E. B. Du Bois.[11] Carrie Williams Clifford died in 1934 five years after the stock market crash and at the close of the Harlem Renaissance.[12]

In many ways Clifford's poetry bridges the civil rights strategies of the 1960s and those of her nineteenth-century predecessors. She foreshadows Martin Luther King Jr. and Shelby Steele when she raises the issue of race versus character in such poems as "My Baby" and "Character or Color—Which?" At the same time, in poems such as "Duty's Call" she recalls Maria W. Stewart, her nineteenth-century predecessor, who had issued a call in the 1830s to the "fair daughters of Africa" to do their part in uplifting the race.[13] In "America," the opening poem in *Race Rhymes*, Clifford demands, "Nay, bid me not be dumb— / I will be heard, Christians, I come / to plead with burning eloquence of truth / A brother's cause" (*RR*, 9). In her poetry and in her life, Clifford did indeed speak with a determination and resolve that would not be quenched by America's accommodationist desires for its black constituency. Clifford was unwavering in reminding America of African Americans' contributions of both their blood and labor for the progress of this country and in warning the "boastful, white American[s]" who, as she saw it, must one day account to an avenging God for the offenses committed against blacks and other people of color (*RR*, 9–10).

Until recently considerably less was known about the life of Carrie Law Morgan Figgs (1878–1968). The daughter of Reverend James Morgan and Lucinda Linton Morgan,[14] Figgs was born on February 3, 1878, in Valdosta, Georgia.[15] Figgs attended grammar school in Valdosta, and high school in Palatka, Florida, and was a graduate of Edward Waters College, an A.M.E. Church-affiliated college in Jacksonville, Florida. While living in Jacksonville, Figgs joined the now historic Mount Zion African Methodist Episcopal Church and married William M. Figgs, a porter.[16] The 1914 Jacksonville city directory lists Figgs as a teacher at Stanton Grade School, boarding at 1014 Julia Street, where she lived with her husband[17] and three children: Leonard, Cassius, and Gwendolyn. Figgs taught in the Jacksonville public schools for twenty-one years.

In the 1910s and 1920s Jacksonville was a bustling city with a prosperous black middle class and a highly upwardly mobile black community. A proud Figgs boasts in a poem addressed to her fellow A.M.E. conferees meeting in the city that they should enjoy all that Jacksonville has to offer; in another poem dedicated to the merchants of Jacksonville, she extolls the city's black doctors, lawyers, restaurateurs, hotel owners, and other merchants, women as well as men, who have made the city outstanding. In "Tribute to the Business Men of Jacksonville," Figgs claims that Jacksonville is one of the places "[w]here the Negro has climbed the hill" (*PP*, 14).

In 1920 Figgs moved from Jacksonville to Chicago, where she became an active member of Bethel A.M.E. Church on 45th and South Michigan. In *Nuggets of Gold*, her second collection of poetry published in 1921, she laments her exchange of the trees, fruit, and sunshine of Florida for the cold climate of Chicago. The 1923 Chicago city directory lists her as residing with her three children, Leonard A., a music teacher; Cassius W., a musician; and Gwendolyn M.,[18] at 528 E. 46th Place. After establishing herself in Chicago, Figgs became a successful businessperson and entrepreneur, founding the Commonwealth Real Estate Employment Company, which she operated from the basement of her home at 4105 S. Park.[19] Affectionately known to her fami-

ly and friends as "Mama Figgs," she was sought out for her saga-
cious advice on matters of propriety, elocution, and decorum.[20]
Just over a month after the assassination of Dr. Martin Luther
King, Figgs died at her home in Chicago on May 14, 1968.

Like that of her contemporary Clifford, Figgs's life illustrates
1920s black women's concerns with duty, service, and uplift. As
an educator in the thriving black community of Jacksonville,
Florida, during the 1910s and 1920s, Figgs often chose drama and
verse to convey her message. An active member of Mount Zion
A.M.E. Church, she was a leader of women's groups, such as the
Women's Mite Missionary Society,[21] a national organization devoted to Christian ideals and racial uplift. Figgs's leadership in black
women's religious organizations was exemplary: as the Grand
Most Ancient Matron of the Heroines of Jericho, an organization
to which only the wives of Masons could belong,[22] she was an
important force among women's groups in the black community.
Her life, like Clifford's, might best be understood within the tradition of black women educators and religious leaders of the 1910s
and 1920s in the South. Both Figgs and Clifford took seriously
their leadership roles within the black community in what was
then described as the dawning of a new era of African-American
and American history.

BLACK WOMEN TEACHERS OF THE LATE NINETEENTH
AND EARLY TWENTIETH CENTURIES

Cynthia Neverdon-Morton, in *Afro-American Women of the
South and the Advancement of the Race, 1895–1925*, maintains
that black women teachers lifted the race through their teaching in
rural as well as urban black communities.[23] According to
Neverdon-Morton,

> The teacher was expected to set an example for the students by
> being neat, prompt, and consistent in her behavior. The tasks were
> formidable ones, requiring more funds than were allocated by the
> states and more energy than it seemed humanly possible to expend.
> (Neverdon-Morton, 80)

Even so, black women teachers of the South persevered in spite of the formidable expectation that they not only teach, but also organize the black community and establish School Improvement Leagues (Neverdon-Morton, 79). Undaunted by overwhelming obstacles, black women educators "chose instead to concentrate on such positive factors as community involvement, community betterment, and enriching the lives of thousands of black children" (Neverdon-Morton, 103).[24]

Shirley J. Carlson delineates other features of the black woman teacher in her article "Black Ideals of Womanhood in the Late Victorian Era":

> In addition to these expectations, shared with the larger society, a black schoolteacher was admired for other characteristics. Usually single, she was an economically independent woman praised first and foremost for her intellectual attainment and assistance to the race. Thus, the teacher not only assisted in educating the young, the role emphasized by the larger culture, but she was also essential to the 'uplift' of the entire black community. (Carlson, 65)

Clifford recognized the importance of her position as teacher/role model in the black community of Parkersburg, West Virginia. After her marriage and subsequent move to Washington, D.C., her appreciation for quality education and teaching increased. In "To Howard University" (WL, 7) Clifford presents Howard University as a black mother with "full breasts" nursing her "children," who are "hungry" for an education, doing so without "turn[ing] a single thirsting soul away."[25] As the speaker makes plain in the poem, thanks should equally "go winging up to God—and You! [Howard University]" (WL, 7).

Clifford reveals her debt to Du Bois in poems like "Within the Veil"[26] and elaborates similar concerns about how to move the race forward in the twentieth century. However, she specifically targets women as her audience in poems like "Duty's Call" (RR) and "Marching to Conquest" (RR), which call on black women to provide the model of service and duty to the African-American community. Stating in the Preface to Race Rhymes that the theme of the collection is "the uplift of humanity," Clifford "calls out" white men for their injustices to blacks in such poems as "Atlanta's Shame,"[27] "Character or Color—Which?," and "My Baby" (RR), making plain the relationship she sees between decrying injustice and achieving progress, in contrast to notable black male leaders at the turn of the century.[28] Nor is she reticent about defying white male power and privilege. In "The Birth of a Nation" Clifford calls D. W. Griffith[29] a "vain, deluded" "rash, misguided fool," ending the poem with a strong warning that such vilification of blacks may result in the blacks' retaliation of "hate for hate" (WL, 40). In "Peril" she likens prejudice to a "foul, festering" "sore" (WL, 11) and in "Race-Hate," penned on the occasion of the East Saint Louis Riot,[30] she warns white Americans that "judgment on thine acts doth wait" (WL, 15). In "Prayer for Deliverance" she asks God to "[f]lay and spare not" the enemies of African Americans (41). Clifford also includes two poems about the Jim Crow laws prevalent in the American South. In "The Jim Crow Car," she maintains that "[n]ot worth but color designates the place where one / must ride" (RR, 13). Whether one achieves the prominence of a Booker T. Washington or becomes a common criminal, if you are a black American, you must suffer the indignity of riding in the "Jim Crow cage." Though she refuses to accept the injustices she experiences in America, Clifford invokes the consolation of black spirituality by conjuring a heaven where "There'll be no caste distinctions" (RR, 14).

In "Shall We Fight the Jim Crow Car?" Clifford denounces injustice against African Americans even more strenuously. In stanza two the speaker states, "Mounts the hot blood to the forehead, / Angry passions leap to life / At remembered wrongs committed / 'Gainst a mother, sister, wife." Like her contemporary Ida B. Wells, Clifford also expresses concern about the destruction of the race via lynching, warning her readers against racist appeals based on what she saw as the imagined potential victimization of white women. Her response to the question presented in the title is a resounding "Yes!"

Clifford highlights the value of struggle as she demonstrates her love of black history as well as her extensive knowledge of

American history in poems like "Lines to Garrison" and "Foraker and the 25th."[31] She celebrates the leadership and achievements of such black American notables as Paul Laurence Dunbar and Frederick Douglass, as well as those of white sympathizers such as John Brown and Harriet Beecher Stowe. In "We'll Die for Liberty" she anticipates Claude McKay's "If We Must Die" (1919) even as she reminds us of the white liberal protagonist at the end of William Wells Brown's play *The Escape* (1858), who chooses to fight for freedom. The poem includes a line from "John Brown's Body," replacing the original "freedom from slavery" with "Equal rights and equal justice, equal opportunity."

Ever conscious of perfecting her art, Clifford handwrote changes to her text,[32] replacing "America is *not* another name for opportunity / To all her sons!" with "America! famed land of liberty / Is not another name for opportunity / To all her sons!" in the poem "America," and revising "Satan's angels" as "Satan's minions" in her "A Reply to Thos. Dixon."[33]

Although both Clifford and Figgs wrote poems about "marching" for the progress of African Americans, Clifford's poetry tends to be more political than Figgs's more subdued verse. In "The Negro's Upward Flight" Figgs proclaims that the African American

>   . . . has flown from his cabin
>   His banjo and pranks
>   To position and honor
>   To title and rank
>   . . . .
>   He is not begging for favors
>   Along so called social lines
>   He wants equal rights
>   For this only, he pines.
>   (*NG*, 16–17)

This poem presents the black conservative ideology, represented by such contemporaries as Booker T. Washington, that promotes the notion of lifting oneself up by one's bootstraps.[34] Figgs proffers the following advice for success in "Elbowing":

INTRODUCTION

This world is a great busy thoroughfare,
To succeed you must elbow your way,
If you wait for success to come to you,
You'll wait there and die in dismay.

(PP, 22)

The literary productions of Clifford and Figgs are framed by the black literary renaissances of the 1890s[35] and the 1920s. Influenced by the renaissance of black women's writing in the 1890s via the work of such women as Anna Julia Cooper,[36] Pauline Hopkins, and Emma Kelley-Hawkins, Clifford and Figgs situate their writing at the cusp of two important black literary movements. As Lorraine Roses and Ruth Elizabeth Randolph demonstrate in *Harlem Renaissance and Beyond: Literary Biographies of 100 Black Women Writers, 1900–1945*, the boundaries or, more specifically, the "edges" of the Harlem Renaissance extended well beyond the physical confines of Harlem, New York, and included such large metropolitan areas as Washington, D.C., Boston, Chicago, and Cleveland.[37] Though scholars dispute the dates of its beginning and ending, most place this renaissance of black productivity in literature, visual arts, and music between 1919 and 1931. Although more has been written about the contributions of black male artists, critics, and literary writers of the Harlem Renaissance, recent scholarship has uncovered a fecund period of black women's productivity in such diverse areas as literature, theatre, dance, visual arts, and music.[38] As an important part of this movement, teacher/poet/playwrights like Figgs penned church and community-based dramas that critique even as they showcase the domestic realm in which the black woman of the early twentieth century found herself situated. Publishing between 1911 and 1923, Clifford and Figgs might best be seen as precursors to the Harlem Renaissance, foregrounding the concerns of the black woman teacher/activist as exemplified by the work of such black women writers of the 1910s and 1920s as Alice Dunbar-Nelson, Georgia Douglas Johnson, Mary Burrill, Myrtle Smith Livingston, and Marita Bonner.[39]

The black woman teacher functioned within the black community both as an agent for political change and as a model of social

xxiii

decorum. But her significance extends beyond these roles, for it was she who began to level the gender playing field within her community by challenging the prescribed gender roles in United States society. The black woman teacher frequently wrote the proverbial book on effective public speaking and deportment, showing to the world through her very existence what the slightest portion of an opportunity for advancement could produce.

THE CULT OF TRUE (BLACK) WOMANHOOD

During the early part of the twentieth century, changing demographics and desires of their audience proved central to how these writers' texts were received. Many works by black women during the 1910s and 1920s were written as entries for literary contests in the NAACP's *Crisis* and the Urban League's *Opportunity* or for women's journals such as *The Birth Control Review*, which were devoted to specific issues affecting women. The audience for these women writers at this point in African-American literary history was that of a literate, predominately black middle class, from porters and domestics to teachers and businesspersons.[40] In an era when a United States president would not only endorse but actually screen with his cabinet a racially defamatory film such as D. W. Griffith's *The Birth of a Nation*,[41] and in which African Americans—men, women, and children—were lynched for dubious crimes, these black women's voices were quite literally crucial for the preservation of the race.

Figgs and Clifford were models of Shirley Carlson's description of "Black Victoria." While delineating specific qualities of "Black Victoria"[42] such as her "virtuous" and "modest" personality and her meticulous care to dress decorously—values shared by the larger American society—Carlson also develops specific instances of difference between late nineteenth-century black and white cultural communities:

> But Black Victoria had other qualities: qualities which were emphasized by her own black community. First and foremost, she was intelligent and well-educated. She displayed a strong community

and racial consciousness, often revealed in her work—whether paid or unpaid—within the black community. Self-confident and outspoken, she was highly esteemed by her community which frequently applauded her as a "race woman" and role model for young people. In these areas, the black community's expectations of the ideal woman differed from those of the larger society." (Carlton, 62)

Clifford's picture on the frontispiece of the volume suggests that Clifford was a model for feminine propriety: the high-collared dress with its ornate beadwork and her long, thick hair lifted in a soft but professional style present a picture of a woman who might have been used by Carlson and others as a prototype for "Black Victoria." More telling is the subtle irony in Clifford's dispersal of daffodils throughout her text: the flowery drawings preceding the poems are undercut by the searing indictment of racism in America presented in the subsequent words.

Similarly, Figgs, the daughter of a late nineteenth-century black minister, understood (ostensibly at least) black communal desire for women to represent virtue in manner as well as in appearance, and she fashioned herself to be just such a model for the black community. An exemplar of womanly decorum, Figgs was described by her Jacksonville contemporary M. M. Holloway thus: "[t]he Grand Most Ancient Matron is a cultured woman[,] unassuming and appro[a]chable at all times[.] [She is] . . . a teacher . . . in the city schools, and is held in high esteem by those who know her."[43]

Devotees of the cult of true black womanhood placed great emphasis on the majesty of the black woman, referring to her often as a "queen." This strong commitment to reimagining black women as positive forces within the black community is evinced in Figgs's own dedication to *Poetic Pearls*, in which she "lovingly" acknowledges her mother's influence, and in her poem "To My Mother," where she not only describes her mother as "the queenliest woman on earth," emphasizing the value of childbearing and teaching, but also likens a mother's love to the provocative, redemptive love of Jesus (5).[44] Throughout her poetry, Figgs values "purity" and "good character" and presents as models for young black women "heroines" "strong and bold," such as the biblical characters Rahab, the "scarlet woman" who assisted Joshua, and Esther and Ruth, whom Figgs praises in "Song Dedicated to the Heroines of Jericho" (*PP*, 16–17). Thus "defending [the] name" of black women by preserving their dignity and moral nature becomes foremost in Figgs's writing. In "The Meanest Man on Earth," for instance, she berates men who "rob" women of the "sacred treasure" (*PP*, 11) "of [their] honor" (*PP*, 10), a theme she continues in "Lamentations of a Deceived Woman" (*PP*, 12–13). In "The Black Queen" (*NG*, 19) Figgs salutes the "honest dusky maid" and proclaims that she be "crown[ed] . . . queen of all":

> In all pure womanly qualities,
>   She stands serene and tall
>
> . . . .
> She answers duty's call.
>   (*NG*,19)

Figgs's concern with promoting strong moral propriety among the black constituency she serves is also shown in her emphasis on temperance. In "A Temperance Poem" (*NG*, 21) she warns her readers against excess, especially in the consumption of alcohol. But it is to the figure of the mother that Figgs looks for the overarching symbol of dignity blended with nurture: in the image of the mother Figgs sees a profound metaphor of America as her most progressive and democratic self, a metaphor that by extension is suggestive of black women's roles in the cradling of American society. As she writes in "The Negro Has Played His Part":

> America, dear America,
>   Mother of all Americans thou art
> You need not grieve, your black boy won't leave
>   He's going to stay and continue to do his part.
>   (*PP*, 16)

Hence, America-as-mother-incarnate must come to understand that though her black children have not been suckled from her breasts as abundantly as her white children, she still retains the love and devotion of her black children—a sentiment reminiscent of those found in Washington's autobiography, *Up from Slavery*.

In addition to her emphasis on temperance and motherhood, Figgs also promotes hard work and thrift as ways for blacks to rise "up from their bootstraps," the salvo with which she concludes *Nuggets of Gold* in "Smile, Work, and Sing." In poems such as "Why Slight the Working Girl?" (*PP*, 8), Figgs underscores the values of work, thriftiness, and making an honest living. Figgs interweaves class as well as race in this poem about a black woman who works to lift herself from poverty.[45]

> Every girl hasn't had the same chance,
> Some come from humble homes,
> But they are just as pure and womanly
> As queens upon their thrones.
>
> (*PP*, 9)

And in "A Jewel Pure and Bright" she takes the more traditional line of argument in presenting gender role division.

> If a woman be a woman,
> Walk the path of truth and right
> . . . .
> When you see a sister faltering,
> Catch her, clasp her hand in thine.
>
> (*PP*, 19)

Figgs here suggests black women's communal obligations to assist one another, just as "[l]ifting others as you climb" provides the central theme of her "Welcome Address Delivered to the Seventh Quadrennial Session of the Women's Mite Missionary Society, Oct. 15th, 1919." Similarly, her admonitions to black boys in "Save Your Pennies" to "[s]ave" "a brother sinking . . . help him lift his head" and "[b]e not idle, be not wasteful / But be diligent instead" (*PP*, 19–20) reflect ideas that she develops in "My Brother's Keeper" (*PP*, 23).

Along with thrift and fortitude, Figgs extolls cleanliness in her poetry and plays. In "Hannah" Figgs praises Hannah for keeping an immaculate home, being of good character, and being clean in appearance. Since physical attractiveness is valued by black devotees of the cult, the speaker describes Hannah as being a "tantalizing brown" (*PP*, 24).

While Clifford might have selected W. E. B. Du Bois as her political mentor and role model for her own activism in the 1910s and 1920s, Figgs clearly identified Booker T. Washington's emphasis on thrift, cleanliness, and self-uplift as the answer to the more immediate needs of a poor, black, Southern constituency. She praised the black independent spirit, embodied by black businessmen and -women of Jacksonville and urged black boys and girls and men and women to be moral and industrious achievers. According to Figgs's logic, America could not continue to ignore African-American initiative if African Americans themselves actualized their fullest potential.

Clifford also reveals a strong commitment to service and duty in her two volumes of poetry, as well as in her published articles and essays. In "All Hail! Ye Colored Graduates," in *Race Rhymes*, her first collection of poetry, Clifford sees service as the unspoken rule of black social and economic mobility. Written so that it might be sung to the tune of "All Hail the Power of Jesus' Name," the poem declares,

> May high ideals each life inspire
> And *service* be its rule
> . . . .
> You'll find the fields for harvest ripe,
> But laborers very few.
> (*RR*, 21)

Clifford lifts the line "You'll find the fields of harvest ripe, / But laborers very few" from a religious song. It is significant that in such poems that focus on service to the race, she frequently addresses women (i.e., "Duty's Call," and "Marching To Conquest") as if she believes that it is up to women to save the race/nation.

Clifford's emphasis on serving one's community by reaching out to those less fortunate reveals a distinct feature of the cult of true black womanhood: black women of the nineteenth and early twentieth centuries were expected to act as role models in a public setting. According to Shirley Carlson, each black woman devotee of the cult was

> [m]orally unassailable, she was virtuous and modest. Her personality was amiable—or "sweet" to use black parlance—she was also altruistic and pious. In appearance she was well groomed and presentable at all times. Her hair was carefully arranged and her costume was immaculate and appropriate for the occasion. In public she wore the traditional Victorian attire: A floor-length dress, with fitted bodice, a full skirt, and long sleeves often trimmed with a ruffle or lace. For formal wear, she would likely don a low-cut gown, which might reveal a considerable portion of her "neck." The ever present hanky with tatted or crotcheted trim displayed her delicate taste and her ability at fine needlework. In all these attributes, Black Victoria upheld the expectations of "true womanhood" which were shared by the larger society. She was a "lady." (Carlton, 62)

It is important to note the extent to which the cult of true [black] womanhood informed and inspirited Clifford's articles and essays as well as her poetry. For instance, in her pithy column in the *Crisis* (1915), Clifford puts the case for enfranchising women plainly:

> When the fact is considered that woman is the chosen channel through which the race is to be perpetrated; that she sustains the most sacred and intimate communion with the unborn babe; that later, she understands in a manner truly marvelous (and explain [*sic*] only by that vague term "instinct") its wants and its needs, the wonder grows that her voice is not the *first* heard in planning for the ideal State in which her child, as future citizen, is to play his part. . . . At his mother's knee the child gets his first impression of love, justice and mercy; and by obedience to the laws of the home he gets his earliest training in civics. (Emphasis in original)[46]

In this article addressing the significance of suffrage for black and white women in view of the dawning of a new era for America,

Clifford equates enfranchising women with progress. The vote for women, according to Clifford, is necessary because the right to vote has become

> [t]he sign of power, the means by which things are brought to pass.
> . . . Why should she be forced to use *indirect* methods to accomplish a thing that could be done so much more quickly and satisfactorily by the direct method—by casting her own ballot?" (*Crisis*, 185 [Emphasis mine])

Clifford's attraction for and appeal to the influence of the cult of true black womanhood appears elsewhere in her poetry, but both Clifford and Figgs find black women's spirituality an equally strong sphere of influence in their responses to the welfare of the black community.

BLACK WOMEN'S JESUS

> Stony the road we trod,
> Bitter the chastening rod,
> Felt in the days when hope unborn had died;
> Yet with a steady beat
> Have not our weary feet
> Come to the place for which our fathers sighed?
> —James Weldon Johnson (1900)

James Weldon Johnson speaks of the African-American predicament at the dawn of what he and other black men and women saw as a new era in African-American history. This "stony road" and "bitter" "chastening rod" have historically led African Americans to mold and exculpate from Western Christianity a religion that could provoke a zeal for liberation even as it evoked a joy in life itself.[47] Jacqueline Grant identifies God as figured in African-American religious experience with specific concerns of black women. In *White Women's Christ and Black Women's Jesus*, Grant argues that "[w]hen Black women say that God is on the side of the oppressed, we mean that God is in solidarity with the struggles of those on the underside of humanity" (Grant, 209). According to Grant, "the daily struggles of poor Black women must serve as a gauge for the verification of the claims of womanist theology" (Grant, 210). Furthermore, describing the "two-fold" nature of black women's spirituality, Grant avers that

> [t]he understanding of God as creator, sustainer, comforter, and liberator took on life as [black women] agonized over their pain, and celebrated the hope that as God delivered the Israelites, they would be delivered as well. The God of the Old and New Testament became real in the consciousness of oppressed Black women. (211)

Grant notes an "interplay of scripture and experience" (211) in the writings of nineteenth-century black women preachers like Jarena Lee, who "engag[ed] the biblical message" and for whom Jesus was "all things," including their "divine co-sufferer, who empowers them in situations of oppression." According to Grant,

> [nineteenth-century Christian Black women] identified with Jesus because they believed that Jesus identified with them. As Jesus was persecuted and made to suffer undeservedly, so were they. His suffering culminated in the crucifixion. Their crucifixion included rape, and babies being sold. (212)

Grant describes the religious joy that a black woman experiences as "a tough, active love that empowered her to fight more fiercely for the freedom of her people" (214).

Figgs shows the way to achieve this kind of provocative black love in her poem, "I Will Trust in Jesus (Sacred)":

> I will trust him all the way,
> > My friend, my Savior, Jesus.
> Until I reach that "Perfect Day",
> > I will trust in Jesus.
> > > (NG, 24)

The speaker in this poem "will trust in Jesus" because she believes in the maxim "If God be with you, who can be against you?" The speaker's" perfect" trust in God will be rewarded on "that 'Perfect Day'" when she receives her heavenly reward, but this knowledge does not keep her from persisting in her struggle for liberation. It is within this context of inspiriting black people with the zeal for provocative, liberatory struggle that Figgs wrote *Select Plays: Santa Claus Land, Jepthah's Daughter, The Prince of Peace*, and *Bachelor's Convention*, plays written for church audiences.

Clifford also reveals a black womanist religious joy in the poems "Like You" (*WL*, 30), "Prayer for Deliverance" (*WL*, 41), "Son" (*WL*, 45), and "God," in which she conceptualizes a more universal God. Like Johnson in "Lift Every Voice and Sing," Clifford and Figgs aver that no struggle can be successful without the strong spiritual underpinnings of a people. As Figgs puts it in "Christ's Person":

> So pure, so perfect, so holy and divine is Christ that language is incapable of conveying to us a true picture of His personality, nor can any human wisdom conceive its wondrous beauty and perfection. (*PP*, 27–28)

Implicit in a critique of Clifford's poetry and Figgs's poetry and plays must be an understanding of the particular needs of their audiences as well as their abilities to negotiate their audiences. These two teacher/role models understood their audience's desire for a proactive black love that engages Christian faith as well as political activism because they, too, desired a liberatory theology. Realizing the hunger for spiritual nourishment within the African-American community, these writers wove a firm foundation in radical Christianity into the fabric of their poetry and plays.[48]

CONCLUSIONS

Finally, one needs to consider what these two pre–Harlem Renaissance women writers saw as the pedagogic function of poetry and, in Figgs's case, of drama.[49] Why did these women prefer poetry as a medium for instruction? Did the literary influence of poetry extend outside of the university community into the space of the church and schoolroom? These questions linger as one reflects on these writers, considering that the vehicle of their work is, more often than not, less impressive than the tenor. Several explanations come to mind, namely, that getting the message of courage, faith, and fortitude out to as many African-American women and men as possible informed both Clifford's and Figgs's manipulation of the literary genres. Since their audiences might range from the lower middle-class domestic worker and day laborer[50] to the middle-class and upper middle-class teacher and independent businessman and -woman, their work had to speak across class lines within the black community. Their poetry could both introduce men, women, boys, and girls to this genre and challenge them to discover Wheatley, Hammond, and Harper. Their manipulation of the genre created a space for poetry at the margins of discourse beside such religious forms as prayer, song, and spiritual essay. For Clifford and Figgs, poetry augmented spiritual belief rather than replaced it. On one level, their poetry can be seen as their attempt to compose a communal song from the oppressed to their God, whom they saw not only as their Deliverer, but also as their Supreme Co-sufferer.

NOTES TO FIGGS'S POETIC PEARLS, 1920

p. 14. "Tribute to the Business Men of Jacksonville." Following are the professions listed for Figgs's noteworthy men and women as cited in the Jacksonville, Florida, city directories dating from the 1910s to 1920s:

A. L. Lewis—Abram L. Lewis, Afro-American Independent Insurance Co.

J. H. Blodgett—Joseph H. Blodgett, real estate

W. J. Geter—Wyatt J. Geter, People's Shoe Company

B. C. Vanderhorst—Byron C. Vanderhorst, Vice President of People's Shoe Company

W. W. Parker—W. Parker, listed as a grocer in the 1919 city directory

Charles H. Anderson—proprietor of the Fish and Oyster Co.

Joe James—Joseph H. James, Jr., listed in the 1926 edition of the *Negro Blue Book* as a realtor, born in 1892 in Pensacola, Florida, a graduate of Clark University, a member of the Elks, the Knights of Pythias, an African-American mutual aid society, the Masons, the Shriners, American Woodsman, Moose, CALANTHE, and Omega Psi Phi.

J. S. McLane—no listing for 1920; 1919, laborer, possibly another McLane.

Pratt Funeral Home—Lawson L. Pratt, undertaker, 525 W. Beaver.

Mrs. Madison Williams, businesswoman, proprietor, Madison Milliners, Moncrief Ave. (H)

Mrs. Kirkpatrick—possibly wife of George Kirkpatrick, proprietor, Richmond Hotel on Broad Street.

Mrs. Sumpter—too many listings, unable to identify

Mrs. McGill—possibly of McGill's Department Store, 523 Broad Street

p. 28. Women's Mite Missionary Society: Oct. 15, 1919, North Jacksonville, Florida. Figgs was the Grand Most Ancient Matron of the Heroines of Jericho in Jacksonville during the 1910s. The Heroines, modeled after such Old Testament women as Rahab and Ruth, was a "society of which only the wives of Masons are allowed to be members" (Lucy Delaney, *From the Darkness Cometh the Light; or, Struggles for Freedom*, [1891; New York: Oxford University Press, 1988], 62–63).

p. 30. Rev. John Hurst—Bishop, "Right Reverend John Hurst, North Jacksonville, 11th Episcopal Dist." Listed in Rev. Charles Sumner Long, *History of the A.M.E. Church in Florida*. Philadelphia: A.M.E. Book Concern, 1939), and M. M. Holloway, *A Daughter's Memento* (Jacksonville, Fla: Edward Waters College, 1920).

p. 30. Mount Zion Church—Erected in 1870, Mount Zion African Methodist Episcopal Church bears historic tradition for

Jacksonville, Florida. The church suffered severe fire damage in 1901 and is presently located on East Beaver and Newman.

p. 30. Edward Waters College, an A.M.E. Church-affliated college from which Figgs received her degree.

p. 30. Dr. Daniel M. Baxter—Presiding Elder, A.M.E. Church of Florida in the second decade of the twentieth century. Figgs describes Dr. Baxter as "one of the most scholarly presiding elders in the entire connection."

p. 32. "Oh, for a Thousand Tongues to Sing"—song that is typically sung as a part of the African Methodist Episcopal Church Service, usually following "The Summary of the Decalogue."

NOTES TO NUGGETS OF GOLD, 1921

p. 13. St. 4, line 4: typo "semotimes" instead of "sometimes."

NOTES TO CLIFFORD'S RACE RHYMES, 1911

There are some changes made in this pamphlet of poetry that are written by hand. Handwritten: "To Wm. Stanley Braithewaite with sincere Esteem" signed "Carrie W. Clifford."

William Stanley Braithwaite (1878–1962) was born on December 6, 1878, in British Guiana of Barbadian, French, and African descent. A professor of English and American literature at Atlanta University for ten years (c. 1935–1945), he was known as a discoverer and mentor of new talent. He was a contributor to the *Boston Evening Transcript*, the *Forum*, the *Century*, *Scribner's*, and the *Atlantic* and was awarded the Spingarn Medal in 1918. His books of poetry include *Lyrics of Life and Love* (poems, 1904) and *The House of Falling Leaves* (1908). See Benjamin Brawley, *The Negro in Literature and Art in the United States* (New York: Dodd, Mead, and Co., 1934) and *The William Stanley Braithwaite Reader*, ed. Philip Butcher (Ann Arbor: University of Michigan Press, 1972), and Philip Butcher, "William Stanley Braithwaite and the College Language Association," *CLA Journal* 15, no. 2 (December 1971), pp. 117–25.

As does Clifford, Braithwaite interrogates the stereotypical portayal of African Americans in Thomas Dixon's *The Leopard Spots*. On *The Leopard Spots*, Braithewaite writes "[w]ith Thomas Dixon, . . . [the] portraiture here descends from caricature to libel" (Braithewaite, 72–73).

p. 19. "Foraker and the Twenty-Fifth." Chaplain Theophilus G. Steward was the regiment's only black officer. He had served as chaplain to black troops in the Philippines during the Spanish American War and authored *The Story of the American Negro as Slave, Citizen and Soldier* (Colored Co-Operative Publishing Co.). As quoted in Joseph Benson Foraker. *Notes of a Busy Life.* Cincinnati: Stewart and Kidd, 1916.

NOTES TO THE WIDENING LIGHT, 1922

p. 4. "Frederick Douglass." According to William L. Andrews, Douglass was born on "an obscure farm" on the eastern shore of Maryland in 1818.

p. 15. "Race-Hate." Likely a misprint, the Race Riot in East St. Louis took place on July 2, 1917.

pp. 16–18. "Silent Protest Parade." The NAACP and other black organizations in New York and other cities held a "Silent Protest Parade" to exert pressure on President Wilson to take action against the violence against black citizens in East St. Louis. See Ralph Ginzburg, *100 Years of Lynchings* (1962; Baltimore: Black Classic Press, 1988, 104–6) and David Levering Lewis, *W. E. B. Du Bois: Biography of a Race, 1868–1919* (New York: Henry Holt, 1993).

pp. 19–20. "Little Mother." Mary Turner's lynching: Ralph Ginzburg lists a Mary Turner and a Hayes Turner as having been lynched in Brooks and Lowndes Counties, Georgia, on May 17, 1918. Ralph Ginzburg, *100 Years of Lynchings* (1962; Baltimore: Black Classic Press, 1988), 260.

p. 24. "Ethopia shall stretch forth her hand." Psalm 68: 31, "Ethiopia shall soon stretch out her hands unto God."

p. 40. *The Birth of a Nation.* D. W. Griffith's *The Birth of a Nation* premiered at the Liberty Theater in New York, March 3, 1915. See note to "A Reply to Thos. Dixon," *RR*, p. 11.

NOTES

[1] I would like to thank the following librarians for their kind assistance: especially Mary Ann Cleveland, Florida Collection, State Library of Florida; Joan Morris, Photographic Collection, Florida State Archives; Donna Wells and Janet Sims-Wood, Moorland-Spingarn Research Center; Ms. Brugger and Mr. Phil Slocum, Genealogy Department of the Main Library, Jacksonville Public Library; individuals from the Jacksonville, Florida, and Chicago, Illinois, communities: Rev. T. E. Shehee, Jacksonville, Florida; Ms. Winifred Small, Mount Zion A.M.E. Zion Church, Jacksonville, Florida; Mrs. Frances McKinney; Bethel A.M.E. Church in Chicago, Illinois; and my sincere thanks to Florida H. Figgs (Mrs. Cassius) for generously sharing information contained in her mother-in-law's, Carrie Figgs, eulogy with me. We can now speak with confidence about Figgs's parents, her place of birth, and other essential facts about her life and contributions to society. Also, I would like to thank my colleague Pat O'Donnell for reading a draft of this text.

[2] Shirley J. Carlson. "Black Ideals of Womanhood in the Late Victorian Era," *Journal of Negro History* 77, no. 2 (1992): 61–73.

[3] Jacqueline Grant. *White Women's Christ and Black Women's Jesus: Feminist Christology and Womanist Response* (Atlanta: Scholar's Press, 1989). This will be developed later in the introduction.

[4] Cynthia Neverton-Morton. *Afro-American Women of the South and the Advancement of the Race, 1895–1925* (Knoxville: University of Tennessee Press, 1989), 103.

[5]Carrie W. Clifford, *Race Rhymes* (Washington, D.C.: Pendleton, 1911), 7.

[6]Scholars may speculate whether Clifford saw parallels in the timing of her birth and the end of the slave era: three years before, John Brown had waged his famous raid on Harper's Ferry, and one year after her birth, Frederick Douglass would issue a call to young free black men of the North to join the Union Army and help quell the forces of slavery in the South.

[7]Clifford's granddaughter is in the process of writing a biography of her grandmother.

[8]Clifford seems to have been very close to her mother. In her dedication to *Race Rhymes*, Clifford writes, "Mother, Mother, how I loved thee! / And I know thou lov'dst me well."

[9]The National Convention of Colored Citizens at which Frederick Douglass spoke convened there in 1848. See Howard Holman Bell, *Minutes of the Proceedings of the National Negro Conventions, 1830–1864* (New York: Arno, 1969), 9–10. The "Report of the Proceedings of the Colored National Convention, Held at Cleveland, Ohio, Wednesday, September 6, 1848" states that the delegates to the convention passed an amendment to send a vote of thanks to the citizens of Cleveland for its hospitality to the convention, with the exception of Mr. Alexander Bowman of the steamboat *Saratoga*, who had refused a black delegate passage in the cabin of his ship.

[10]Carrie W. Clifford. "Cleveland and Its Colored People." *Colored American Magazine* 8–9 (1908): 380.

[11]*Harlem Renaissance and Beyond: Literary Biographies of 100 Black Women Writers, 1900–1945*, ed. Lorraine Elena Roses and Ruth Elizabeth Randolph (Boston: G. K. Hall, 1990).

[12]The Cliffords were active members of the NAACP, an organization forged from the alliances of the black "talented tenth" and white liberals. By the time of Carrie Clifford's death, the organization had become a formidable force in the advocacy of civil rights in America. See Mary White Ovington, "How the National Association for the Advancement of Colored People Began" (*Crisis* [1914; January 1989]: 38–42) and *W. E. B. Du Bois Speaks*, ed. Philip S. Foner (New York: Pathfinder, 1979), 23–25.

[13]Maria W. Stewart, "Religion and the Pure Principles of Morality, the Sure Foundation on Which We must Build," in *Maria W. Stewart, America's First Black Woman Political Writer*, ed. Marilyn Richardson (Bloomington: Indiana University Press, 1987).

[14]According to the earliest references to Figgs in the Jacksonville, Florida, city directory, by the end of the nineteenth century when her family had moved there from Georgia, Figgs's mother Lucinda Morgan (b. 1863) had remarried William Wright (b. 1862), stepfather to Figgs. Figgs was the oldest of four daughters, with sisters Nancie V. (b. 1883), Gertrude (b. 1888), and Mamie (b. 1890).

[15]Confirming by telephone and by the letter of eulogy, Mrs. F. H. Figgs provided me with this information about Figgs's birth (Mrs. Florida H. Figgs, private conversation, February 4, 1995). The Florida Census Soundex Film for 1900 had shown a discrepancy about Figgs's birthplace as Georgia or Florida. Thanks to C. H. Harris, librarian with the Florida Collection of the Jacksonville Public Libraries, for calling this to my attention.

[16]This information is contained in the eulogy for Carrie L. M. Figgs, who died in 1968, handcopied by Mrs. Florida H. Figgs.

[17]Various Jacksonville city directories from 1899 to 1917 list Figgs as Carrie Morgan, a laundress in 1899, living at 1215 Pippin; the wife of William Figgs, a porter, living at 1452 Franklin in 1902; a teacher at Lewisville School in 1908; a teacher at W. Lewisville School in 1910, living at 1014 Julia; and a teacher at Stanton Grade School in 1914. Her last listing is in the 1917 Jacksonville city directory as a teacher at Stanton School, living at 1014 Julia.

[18]Leonard A. Figgs was blind.

[19]Now Martin Luther King Drive.

[20]Frances McKinney, Figgs's niece-in-law, related a story of how she and others sought out her aunt's advice on speech preparations, etc. (Frances McKinney, private conversation, September 21, 1994).

[21]Mary A. Certain and Mary Frisby Handy were two of the organizers of the Women's Mite Missionary Society in Jacksonville, Florida, later to be renamed the Women's Home and Foreign Missionary Society when Bishop Flipper was sent to Florida. See Rev. Charles Sumner Long, comp., *History of the A.M.E. Church in Florida* (Philadelphia: A.M.E. Book Concern, 1939), 118.

[22]According to M. M. Holloway, the Heroines of Jericho began with the African Lodge #459 of Massachusetts and with the history of freemasonry in America since 1764. M. M. Holloway, *A Daughter's Memento* (Jacksonville, Fla: Edward Waters College Press, 1920), 34–36. Holloway includes a clipping from a notice in the *Times-Union* describing the 32d anniversary of the Heroines of Jericho held at the Masonic Temple, at which Figgs presided as Grand Most Ancient Matron (Holloway, 33–37). Figgs is listed on the program as an officer of "the Most Worshipful Grand Court of Heroines of Jericho, 1914" (Holloway, 37).

[23]Cynthia Neverdon-Morton, *Afro-American Women of the South and the Advancement of the Race, 1895–1925* (Knoxville: University of Tennessee Press, 1989).

[24]For more information about the valuation of teaching and racial uplift among blacks in the South, see Arnold Cooper, *Between Struggle and Hope: Four Black Educators in the South, 1894–1915* (Ames: Iowa State University Press, 1989).

[25]Clifford's maternal imagery conjoins Toomer in imaging America as the fair babe nursed by the black woman's breasts in *Cane* and prefigures Morrison's representation of Sethe in *Beloved.*

[26]Clifford had read Du Bois's *The Souls of Black Folk.* The subtitle of "My Baby" is "(*On Reading 'Souls of Black Folk'*)." David Levering Lewis notes a letter from Du Bois to Carrie Clifford when he was recuperating from kidney surgery (525); the letter, W. E. B. Du Bois to Carrie W. Clifford, is dated January 29, 1917, and is held with the Du Bois Papers/University of Massachusetts as cited in David Levering Lewis, *W. E. B. Du Bois: Biography of a Race, 1868–1919* (New York: Holt, 1993), 690.

[27]"Atlanta's Shame" (*RR,* 12) is likely an allusion to the Atlanta race riot that took place on September 22, 1906, in which 10,000 whites attacked all blacks in sight, raiding train stations, trolley cars, post offices, etc. in search of African Americans to assault. Read with "A Reply to Thos. Dixon," the two poems represent a sustained critique of racism and lynching in the United States. For further information on the race riot in Atlanta, see the Atlanta *Constitution* ("Atlanta Is Swept by Raging Mob," September 23, 1906, p. 1; "Negroes Attack Inman Park," September 23, 1906, p. 3; "State Troops Quiet Atlanta," September 24, 1906, p. 1; "Peace in Atlanta Till Night Brought Blood in Suburbs," September 25, 1906, p. 1); Ray Stannard Baker, *The Atlanta Riot* (issued by the Afro American Council, 1907) as quoted in David Levering Lewis, *W. E. B. Du Bois: A Biography of a Race* (New York: Holt, 1993); and Joel Williamson, *The Crucible of Race: Black-White Relations in the American South since Emancipation* (New York: Oxford University Press, 1984), 209–23. There had also been a race riot in Atlanta six years previously, recorded in the *New York Times* as "Race Riot in Georgia" (*New York Times,* 18 August 1900), 2.

[28]Like Booker T. Washington, for instance.

[29]Filmmaker D. W. Griffith collaborated with novelist Thomas Dixon in the making of the film *The Birth of a Nation.*

[30]On July 2, 1917, white East St. Louisians, fearful of the threat of job loss, killed and burned black emigres to East St. Louis who had come in search of job opportunities and the promise of greater equality in the North. See Elliott Rudwick, *Race Riot at East St. Louis, July 2, 1917* (New York: Atheneum, 1972), 58–73. This white-on-black riot was one of many scenes of interracial violence that took place during the W W I years. These northern scenes of racial violence coincide with a substantial black migration from the South. The most severe race riot during the W W I period was the East St. Louis riot, in which nine whites and thirty-nine blacks were killed. Allen Grimshaw cites thirty-three "major interracial disturbances" in the United States between 1900 and 1949, eighteen occurring

between 1915 and 1919 (Allen D. Grimshaw, "A Study in Social Violence," Ph.D. diss., University of Pennsylvania, 1959, 178–80, as quoted in Rudwick, 3).

[31]Senator Joseph Benston Foraker of Ohio defended the three black troops (Companies B, C, and D, including some veterans of the Cuban battles cited for their valor) dismissed under the Taft administration as recompense for the alleged behavior of a few black soldiers on a shooting spree in Brownsville, Texas. Foraker's political career was ruined because of his defense of the infantrymen.

[32]Though Clifford was some sixteen years his senior, her handwritten inscription to Race Rhymes, "To Wm. Stanley Braithewaite, With sincere esteem, Carrie W. Clifford," attests to her admiration of this scholar/critic, an admiration similar to the kind of adoration a student has for a beloved teacher, revealing both her desire to pay homage as well as to show pride in her own literary achievements.

[33]Race Rhymes, 9, 11. See Raymond A. Cook, Thomas Dixon (New York: Twayne, 1974).

[34]Figgs also shows her debt to Paul Laurence Dunbar, whose influence via such poems of his as "In the Morning" and "When Malindy Sings" are clearly evident in this poem, as well as in Figgs's "Cane Juice and 'Possum," "Whoa Mule," and "Who's You Talking To."

[35]Anna Julia Cooper, Pauline Hopkins, Frances E. W. Harper, Gertrude B. Mossell, Amelia E. Johnson, Katherine Davis Chapman Tillman, Emma Dunham Kelley-Hawkins, Octavia Albert, and Victoria Earle Matthews are some of the notable women writers of the literary renaissance of the 1890s.

[36]Anna Julia Cooper (1858–1964) is best known as the author of A Voice from the South (1892).

[37]See Lorraine Elena Roses and Ruth Elizabeth Randolph, Harlem Renaissance and Beyond: Literary Biographies of 100 Black Women Writers, 1900–1945 (Boston: G. K. Hall, 1990).

[38]In addition to Roses and Randolph, see also Gloria T. Hull, Color, Sex, and Poetry: Three Women Writers of the Harlem Renaissance (Bloomington: Indiana University Press, 1987), Give Us Each Day: The Diary of Alice Dunbar-Nelson (New York: Norton, 1984), and The Works of Alice Dunbar Nelson (New York: Oxford University Press, 1988); Maureen Honey, ed., Shadowed Dreams: Women's Poetry of the Harlem Renaissance (New Brunswick, N.J.: Rutgers University Press, 1989); Mary Knopf, ed., The Sleeper Wakes: Harlem Renaissance Stories by Women (New Brunswick, N.J.: Rutgers University Press, 1993); and Sona L. Chambers, Sisters of the Harlem Renaissance: The Found Generation, 1920–1932, ed. Gail Cohee and Leslie Lewis

(Martinsville, Ind.: Helaine Victoria Press, 1991), a postcard collection containing photographs with brief biographies of the various vaudeville stars, actors, novelists, sculptors, and other visual artists, journalists, etc. See also the discussion of black women's contributions to the Harlem Renaissance in Darlene Clark Hine, ed., *Black Women in America: An Historical Encyclopedia*, Vol. 1 (New York: Carlson, 1993). William L. Andrews's edition, *Classic Fiction of the Harlem Renaissance* (New York: Oxford University Press, 1994), contains selections by Hurston and Larsen.

[39]Perhaps James Weldon Johnson, their male contemporary and noted African-American writer/scholar, who, like Figgs, had taught at famed Stanton Grade School, had his finger on the pulse of the black teacher's credo of *service* when he writes in his autobiography *Along This Way* of the largess with which black teachers in the South during the early 1900s served their constituency:

> The central idea embraced a term that is now almost a butt for laughter—"service." We were never allowed to entertain any thoughts of being educated as "go-getters." Most of us knew that we were being educated for life work as underpaid teachers. The ideal constantly held up to us was of education as a means of living, not making a living. It was impressed upon us that taking a classical course would have an effect of making us better and nobler, and of higher value to those we should have to serve. An odd, old-fashioned, naive conception? Rather. (James Weldon Johnson, *Along This Way: The Autobiography of James Weldon Johnson* [New York: Viking, 1933], 122)

Born in Jacksonville, Florida, Johnson taught at Stanton immediately after receiving his M.A. degree from Atlanta University in 1904. Under Johnson's administration in the early 1900s, Stanton Grade School expanded into Stanton High School, with Johnson advancing as principal. By the time Figgs was to teach at Stanton, however, it appears that Johnson had already left his position as principal in pursuit of a career as a writer/director of black productions on Broadway and a political career with the NAACP. Unlike his fellow teacher Figgs, Johnson had little tolerance for the secret societies such as the black Masons of Jacksonville. See also Arethenia J. Bates, "James Weldon Johnson 1871–1938," *Heath Anthology of American Literature*, Paul Lauter, gen. ed., vol. 2 (Lexington, Mass.: Heath, 1994), 1033–35.

[40]See Kathy Perkins, *Black Female Playwrights* (Bloomington: Indiana University Press, 1989); James Hatch and Ted Shine, *Black Theater USA* (New York: Free Press, 1974); and Leo Hamalian and James Hatch, *The Roots of African American Drama: An Anthology of Early Plays, 1858–1938* (Detroit: Wayne State University Press, 1991).

[41]As Raymond A. Cook documents it, Thomas Dixon (1864–1946) and Woodrow Wilson had been friends from their days at Johns Hopkins University in 1883, where Dixon attended for one semester. Cementing their fraternal bond, Dixon nominated Wilson for an honorary doctorate at Wake Forest College in 1888. Dixon also became friends with other white male power moguls such as John D. Rockefeller after he moved to New York.

In 1905 Dixon published a novel, *The Clansman*; the play adaptation of the novel toured the United States, meeting with much publicity and sensationalism. The film version of *The Clansman* premiered as *The Birth of a Nation* in 1915, after Dixon first gained audience to and an endorsement of the film from his old friend and then U.S. president Woodrow Wilson and his cabinet, the Supreme Court, and both houses of Congress. The endorsement of the film by President Wilson, his cabinet, and the Supreme Court justices curbed the efforts of African Americans and sympathetic whites to prevent the distribution of the film. See Raymond A. Cook, *Thomas Dixon* (New York: Twayne, 1974), 114–17.

[42]The name Carlton gives to black women who, during the late Victorian era, ascribed to the values of the cult of true womanhood. See Shirley Carlton, "Black Ideals of Womanhood in the Late Victorian Era," *Journal of Negro History* 77, no. 2 (1992): 61–73.

[43]Holloway, 33.

[44]Figgs expresses her own motherly love for her three children, Leonard, Cassius, and Gwendolyn, in *Nuggets of Gold* (*NG*, 9).

[45]This is also the central theme of Mary Burrill's play, *They Sit in Darkness* (1919).

[46]Carrie W. Clifford. "Votes for Children," *Crisis* 10, no. 4 (August 1915): 185.

[47]See Cornel West, *Prophesy Deliverance! An Afro-American Revolutionary Christianity* (Philadelphia: Westminster Press, 1982); James Cone, *God of the Oppressed* (New York: Seabury Press, 1975); Jacqueline Grant, *White Women's Christ and Black Women's Jesus* (Atlanta: Scholars Press, 1988).

[48]See West, *Prophesy Deliverance!*

[49]I am indebted to my colleague Daniel Morris for suggesting these questions in this section of the paper.

[50]This was especially true in the case of Figgs's audience in Jacksonville, Florida.

BIBLIOGRAPHY

Anderson, James Douglas. *Education for Servitude: The Social Purposes of Schooling in the Black South, 1870–1930*. Ann Arbor, Mich.: University Microfilms International, 1973.

Andrews, William, ed. *Classic Fiction of the Harlem Renaissance*. New York: Oxford University Press, 1994.

Bell, Howard Holman. *Minutes of the Proceedings of the National Negro Conventions, 1830–1864*. New York: Arno, 1969.

———. *A Survey of the Negro Convention Movement, 1830–1861*. New York: Arno, 1969.

Brawley, Benjamin. *The Negro in Literature and Art in the United States*. New York: Dodd, Mead, 1934.

Butcher, Philip. "William Stanley Braithwaite and the College Language Association." *CLA Journal* 15, no. 2 (December 1971): 117–125.

———, ed. *The William Stanley Braithwaite Reader*. Ann Arbor: University of Michigan Press, 1972.

Carlson, Shirley J. "Black Ideals of Womanhood in the Late Victorian Era." *Journal of Negro History* 77, no. 2 (1992): 61–73.

Clifford, Carrie Williams. "Cleveland and Its Colored People." *The Colored American Magazine* 8–9 (1908): 365–80.

———. "Love's Way (A Christmas Story)." *Alexander's Magazine* 1, no. 9 (January 1906): 55–58.

———. *Race Rhymes*. Washington, D.C.: Pendleton, 1911.

———. *Sowing for Others to Reap: A Collection of Papers of Vital Importance to the Race*. (Ohio Federation of Colored Women's Clubs, Carrie Williams Clifford, editor). Boston: Alexander, n.d.

———. "Votes for Children," *Crisis* 10, no. 4 (August 1915): 185.

———. *The Widening Light*. Boston: Walter Reid, 1922.

Cone, James. *God of the Oppressed*. New York: Seabury, 1975.

———. *Speaking the Truth: Ecumenism, Liberation and Black Theology*. Grand Rapids, Mich.: Eerdmans, 1986.

Cook, Raymond A. *Thomas Dixon*. New York: Twayne, 1974.

Cooper, Anna Julia. *A Voice from the South*. Intro. Mary Helen Washington. 1892. Reprint. New York: Oxford University Press, 1988.

Cooper, Arnold. *Between Struggle and Hope: Four Black Educators in the South, 1894–1915*. Ames: Iowa State University Press, 1989.

Delaney, Lucy. *From the Darkness Cometh the Light; or, Struggles for Freedom*. 1891. Reprint. New York: Oxford University Press, 1988.

Figgs, Carrie Law Morgan. *Nuggets of Gold*. Chicago: Carrie Law Morgan Figgs, 1921.

———. *Poetic Pearls*. Jacksonville, Fla.: Edward Waters College Press, 1920.

———. *Select Plays: Santa Claus Land, Jepthah's Daughter, The Prince of Peace, and Bachelors' Convention*. Chicago: Carrie Law Morgan Figgs, 1923.

Foner, Eric, ed. *America's Black Past: A Reader in Afro-American History*. New York: Harper & Row, 1970.

Foraker, Joseph Benson. *Notes of a Busy Life*. Cincinnati: Stewart & Kidd, 1916.

Foster, Frances Smith. *Written by Herself: Literary Productions by African American Women, 1746–1892*. Bloomington: Indiana University Press, 1993.

Ginzburg, Ralph. *100 Years of Lynchings*. 1962. Reprint. Baltimore: Black Classic Press, 1988.

Grant, Jacqueline. *White Women's Christ and Black Women's Jesus: Feminist Christology and Womanist Response*. Atlanta: Scholar's Press, 1989.

Higginbotham, Evelyn Brooks. *Righteous Discontent: The Women's Movement in the Black Baptist Church, 1880–1920*. Cambridge, Mass.: Harvard University Press, 1992.

Hine, Darlene Clark, ed. *Black Women in America: An Historical Encyclopedia*. Vol. 1. New York: Carlson, 1993.

Holloway, M. M. *A Daughter's Memento*. Jacksonville, Fla.: Edward Waters College Press, 1920.

Johnson, James Weldon. *Along this Way: The Autobiography of James Weldon Johnson*. 1933. Reprint. New York: Viking, 1968.

Knopf, Marcy, ed. *The Sleeper Wakes: Harlem Renaissance Stories by Women*. New Brunswick, N.J.: Rutgers University Press, 1993.

Lewis, David Levering. *W. E. B. DuBois: Biography of a Race*. New York: Holt, 1993.

Long, Charles Sumner. *History of the A.M.E. Church in Florida*. Philadelphia: A.M.E. Book Concern, 1939.

McFeely, William, *Frederick Douglass*. New York and London: W. W. Norton, 1991.

Meier, August. "Negro Class Structure and Ideology in the Age of Booker T. Washington." In *America's Black Past: A Reader in Afro-*

American History, ed. Eric Foner. New York: Harper & Row, 1970, 266–75.

———. "The Paradox of W. E. B. Du Bois." In *America's Black Past: A Reader in Afro-American History*, ed. Eric Foner. New York: Harper & Row, 1970, 280–97.

Neverdon-Morton, Cynthia. *Afro-American Women of the South and the Advancement of the Race, 1895–1925*. Knoxville: University of Tennessee Press, 1989.

Ovington, Mary White. "How the National Association for the Advancement of Colored People Began," *Crisis* (January 1989): 38–42, 117. (Reprint from *Crisis* 8, no. 4 [August 1914], 184–88.)

Perkins, Kathy. *Black Female Playwrights*. Bloomington: Indiana University Press, 1989.

Preston, Dickson J. *Young Frederick Douglass: The Maryland Years*. Baltimore: Johns Hopkins University Press, 1980.

"Race Riot in Georgia," *New York Times*, 18 August 1900, 2.

Roses, Lorraine Elena, and Ruth Elizabeth Randolph. *Harlem Renaissance and Beyond: Literary Biographies of 100 Black Women Writers, 1900–1945*. Boston: G. K. Hall, 1990.

Salem, Dorothy C., ed. *African American Women: A Biographical Dictionary*. New York and London: Garland, 1993.

Stockbridge, Frank Parker, and John Holliday Perry. *Florida in the Making*. Foreword by Gov. John W. Martin. Kingsport, Tenn.: Kingsport Press, 1926.

Suggs, Henry Lewis, ed. *The Black Press in the South, 1865–1979*. Westport, Conn.: Greenwood, 1983.

Torrence, Ridgely. *Granny Maumee, The Rider of Dreams & Simon the Cyrenian: Plays for a Negro Theater*. New York: Macmillan, 1917.

Watts, Eugene J. *The Social Bases of City Politics: Atlanta, 1865–1903*. Westport, Conn.: Greenwood, 1978.

Weaver, John D. *The Brownsville Raid*. New York: W. W. Norton, 1970.

Williamson, Joel. *The Crucible of Race: Black-White Relations in the American South Since Emancipation*. New York: Oxford University Press, 1984.

RACE RHYMES

BY CARRIE W. CLIFFORD

WASHINGTON, D. C.

1911

CARRIE W. CLIFFORD

RACE RHYMES

—BY—

CARRIE W. CLIFFORD

WASHINGTON, D. C.

1911

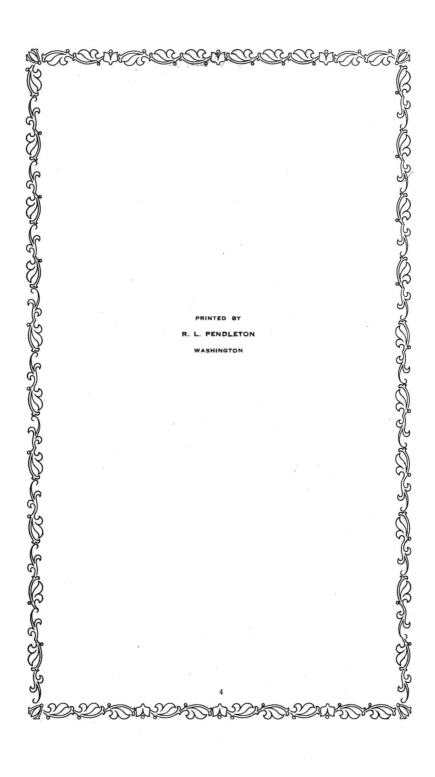

PRINTED BY

R. L. PENDLETON

WASHINGTON

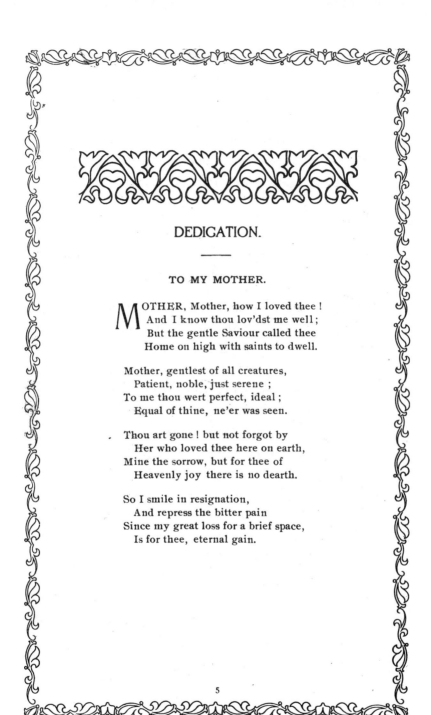

DEDICATION.

TO MY MOTHER.

MOTHER, Mother, how I loved thee !
And I know thou lov'dst me well ;
But the gentle Saviour called thee
Home on high with saints to dwell.

Mother, gentlest of all creatures,
Patient, noble, just serene ;
To me thou wert perfect, ideal ;
Equal of thine, ne'er was seen.

Thou art gone ! but not forgot by
Her who loved thee here on earth,
Mine the sorrow, but for thee of
Heavenly joy there is no dearth.

So I smile in resignation,
And repress the bitter pain
Since my great loss for a brief space,
Is for thee, eternal gain.

6

PREFACE.

 N giving to the world this brochure, the author makes no claim to unusual poetic excellence or literary brilliance. She is seeking to call attention to a condition which she, at least, considers serious. Knowing that this may often be done more impressively through rhyme than in an elegant prose dissertation, she has taken this method of accomplishing the end sought.

Each poem has been called forth by some significant event or condition in the history of the Negro in America. The theme of the group here presented—the uplift of humanity—is the loftiest that can animate the heart and pen of man; the treatment, she trusts, is not wholly unworthy. Remembering the good that has been accomplished by such familiar poems as "The Prisoner for Debt," "The Song of the Shirt," and similar ones, she sends these lines forth with the prayer that they may change some evil heart, right some wrong and raise some arm strong to deliver.

C. W. C.

Contents

RACE RHYMES

AMERICA.

America is *not* another name for opportunity
To all her sons! Nay, bid me not be dumb—
I will be heard. Christians, I come
To plead with burning eloquence of truth
A brother's cause; ay, to demand, forsooth,
The manhood rights of which he is denied;
Too long your pretense have your acts belied.

What has he done to merit your fierce hate?
I charge you, speak the truth; for know, his fate
Irrevocably is bound up with yours,
For good or ill, as long as time endures.
Torn from his native home by ruthless hands,
For centuries he tilled your fruitful lands,
In shameful, base, degrading slavery;
Your humble, patient, loyal vassal, he—
Piling your coffers high with magic gold,
Himself, the while, like cattle bought and sold.

When devastating war stalked through the land,
And dangers threatened you on every hand,
These sons whose color you cannot forgive,
Did freely shed their blood that you might live
A nation, strong and great. And will you then
Continue to debase, degrade, contemn
Your loyal children, while with smiling face
You raise disloyal ones to power and place?

Is race or color crime, that for this cause
You draft against the Negro unjust laws?
Is race or color sin that he should be
For these things treated so outrageously?
O, boastful, white American, beware!
It is the handiwork of God you dare
Thus to despise and He will you repay

9

With generous measure overflowing, yea,
For all the good which in his life you've wrought,
For helpful deed, or kindly, loving thought—
For every act of cruelty you've done,
For every groan which you have from him wrung,
For every infamy by him endured,
He will you all repay, be thou assured!
Not here alone ere time shall cease to be,
But likewise There, through all eternity.

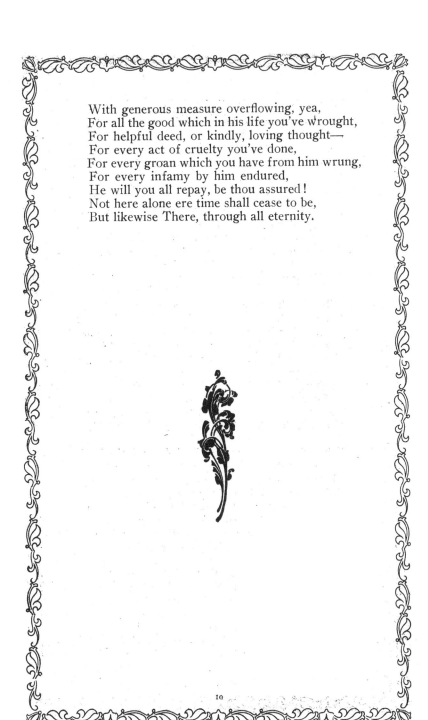

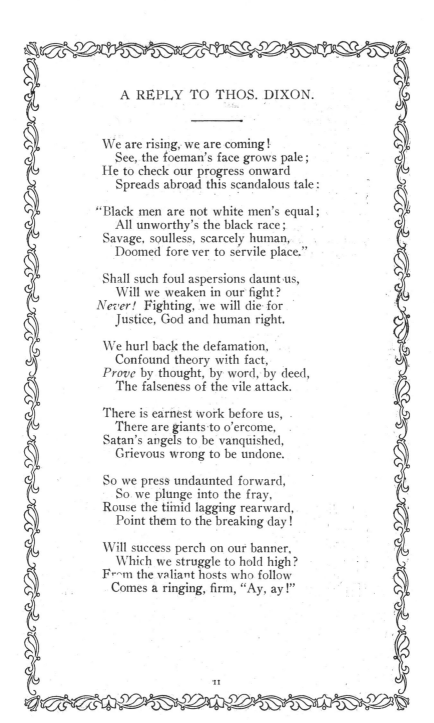

A REPLY TO THOS. DIXON.

We are rising, we are coming!
    See, the foeman's face grows pale;
He to check our progress onward
    Spreads abroad this scandalous tale:

"Black men are not white men's equal;
    All unworthy's the black race;
Savage, soulless, scarcely human,
    Doomed fore ver to servile place."

Shall such foul aspersions daunt us,
    Will we weaken in our fight?
Never! Fighting, we will die for
    Justice, God and human right.

We hurl back the defamation,
    Confound theory with fact,
Prove by thought, by word, by deed,
    The falseness of the vile attack.

There is earnest work before us,
    There are giants to o'ercome,
Satan's angels to be vanquished,
    Grievous wrong to be undone.

So we press undaunted forward,
    So we plunge into the fray,
Rouse the timid lagging rearward,
    Point them to the breaking day!

Will success perch on our banner,
    Which we struggle to hold high?
From the valiant hosts who follow
    Comes a ringing, firm, "Ay, ay!"

ATLANTA'S SHAME.

In queenly state she sits at the gateway of the South—
  And lifts with conscious pride her stately head:
Fair Atlanta feels her worth, and her children are elate,
  As thro' her streets they go with happy tread.

She has sons of many kinds, she has sons of many hues,
  And she says she cares for all, but this we know,
Tho' she exacts of each alike service, revenue, respect,
  The blacks get of her favor but scant show!

Yet the harder do they strive her good will and grace
      to win,
  Keeping step with progress—forward without pause!
Gaining knowledge, getting wealth, doing all things
      duly meet,
  Hoping thus to gain Atlanta's prized applause.

But alas! 'tis all in vain, for she hates with bitter hate
  These poor blacks who aye remind her of her shames;
Of her greed for wealth and power, of her base con-
    suming lust:
Noble striving but the more her wrath inflames.

Then to hide from honest eyes her blood-guiltiness and
      sin,
  She most cunningly contrives a wicked plot—
Subtly spoken a base word, then this cry against the
      blacks
  Cleaves the night! "Revenge! lynch, slaughter and
    spare not!"

Three awful nights she reveled in a carnival of crime,
  Three days or e'er the tension was relieved;
When her thirst for blood was sated, the whole nation
      stood aghast,
  Her cry of "Rape," no more the world deceived!

Lamentations, bitter sobs, heart-wrung groans the soft
    winds bore
Thro' the streets where lay the victims of her rage;
Helpless age and guiltless youth, innocence and trust-
    ing truth—
It had taken *all,* her fury to assuage.

Dread Atlanta nevermore can the crimson stain erase,
    Nor the foul blot wipe from off fair history's scroll;
This feli deed shall e'er arise, ghost-like from the mists
    of time
To confront and terrify her guilty soul!

THE JIM CROW CAR.

Of all things iniquitous that evil could devise,
A thing that men of honor very justly must despise,
An institution infamous and more degrading far
Than aught I know of, fellow-men, this is the Jim Crow
    car.

The good, the bad, the criminal are herded there
    together;
Just so the skin is dark, no white would deign to ques-
    tion whether
The heart beneath was pure as gold or was with guilt
    allied;
Not worth but color designates the place where one
    must ride.

He may have built, of modern times, the greatest insti-
    tution
For training hands; or may be of the vilest destitution
A perfect sample; but tho' he be artist, brute or sage,
It nothing counts, he goes if black into the "Jim Crow"
    cage.

He may have won prized scholarships from greatest
    schools of learning,
The fire of genius in his soul with mighty brilliance
    burning;
His culture and attainments may indeed be on a par
With earth's greatest souls, but he, if black, must seek
    the "Jim Crow" car.

And shall the strong be e'er deceived with thought that
    might makes right?
And shall the weak forever yield God-given right to
    might?
Nay! think not, puny man, to alter one of God's fixed
    laws,
For sure as darkness follows light, effect must follow
    cause.
And sure as nations disregard God's changeless plan
    divine
To justly deal, show mercy, love and service intertwine,
So surely will his judgment fall with vengeance swift
    and true,
On all who seek to thwart His will, His mandates to
    eschew.

And in His gracious message left to comfort breaking
    hearts
He promises to rescue all from Satan's fiery darts
Who keep His law: there, too, we find the blest assur-
    ance given
There'll be no caste distinctions in the glorious realm of
    heaven.

Nor bond nor free, nor Greek nor Jew, Barbarian,
    Scythian there;
For all are one in Christ, all children of His loving care;
And when at last His little ones have crossed life's
    moaning bar,
They'll ride in golden chariots, not in a "Jim Crow"
    car.

SHALL WE FIGHT THE JIM CROW CAR?

Comes the question, loud, insistent,
Borne upon the winds afar,
In the ears of black men ringing—
"Shall we fight the Jim Crow car?"

Mounts the hot blood to the forehead,
Angry passions leap to life
At remembered wrongs committed
'Gainst a mother, sister, wife.

And the milk of human kindness
In the proud heart turns to gall:
Is not every hand against them,
Every ear deaf to their call?

Disregarded all entreaties,
Stern protests unheeded are;
Impotent words or achievements,
To remove the color-bar.

Shall such base, unworthy treatment
Be by brave men tamely borne
And the title "Non-resistant,"
As a badge of honor worn?

No; by heaven, they swear it, swear it!
List ye, farthest glitt'ring star,
Ten thousand black men shout in chorus,
"We will fight the Jim Crow car."

THE SINGER AND THE SONG.

To Paul Laurence Dunbar.

For oh, his song was so sad to hear!
He sang of the millions who live in fear;
Of those who in anguish and patient pain,
Struggle for freedom but struggle in vain.

For oh, his song was so sweet to hear;
It fell like balm on the listening ear;
It told of bright skies, fragrant flowers, green trees,
And of God the Almighty—Creator of these.

For oh, his song was so blithe and gay,
"I will not hold my just anger alway;
Tremble ye wicked ones!" Assurance blest,
And hope brought the song to these children oppressed.

For oh, his song was sublime, sublime!
A glorious burst of music divine;
"He whose endurance shall last to the end,
On him shall heaven's choicest blessings descend."

So ever he sang as he journeyed along,
Cheering the faint heart, rebuking the wrong,
Preaching to all the sweet gospel of love;
Teaching of Jesus who reigneth above.
But the singer grew weary and sank down to rest,
Where he sleeps for a space, folded close to the breast
Of old Mother Earth, the song stilled for a day,
But our hearts to its music will vibrate alway.

LINES TO GARRISON.

(Read at His Centenary Celebration, Cleveland, Oho.)

Read at his centennary celebration, Cleveland, Ohio.
Ah, dark and grim and direful were those days,
For cursed was our fair land, and torn with cries
And groanings loud and terrible, of man
Oppressed and tortured by his brother man.
The poor, black, naked slave was worked and whipped
And scourged; held, bought and sold as chattel
At the behest of him who styled himself his owner;
His body, mind, yea e'en his very soul
Was held by cruel masters to belong to them!
"How long, O Lord, how long?" wailed these despair-
　　ing ones,
As Slavery's cruel bonds grew stronger day by day,
More loathsome and unbearable!
While thus they agonized in prayer, beseeching
God, the father, for relief from this
Distressed and pitiful estate, lo!
Suddenly from out the mists of chaos
And confusion, rose a voice commanding,
Clear, loud-crying, "I am in earnest—
I will not equivocate—I will not
Retreat a single inch—And I will be heard!"
It was the voice of one who hated slavery
As he hated nothing else on earth;
It was the voice of one, who advocated
Freedom for all men.
It was the voice of Garrison, the brave,
Which sounded clear above the tumult, saying—
"Tyrants as all hist'ry shows, must be destroyed!"
Alarm fell on the sleek, complacent master,
The quiet advocate of abolition likewise started!
Dared he thus boldly agitate for right,
Dared he thus forcibly denounce the wrong?
　　A nation listened breathless!
Again the voice came ringing, firm, emphatic—
"Are we enough to make a revolution?
No, but we are enough, one to begin;
And once begun it cannot be turned back!
I am for revolution, were I utterly alone;
I am there because I must be there;
I cannot choose but obey the voice of God!"

17

It was enough! A Christian nation could not,
Would not listen to the voice of God.
      The South cried for his blood ;
In Boston he was mobbed ; dragged thro' the streets
A rope around his neck, because, forsooth,
He dared to speak for Freedom, Justice, Right.
But brute force cannot thrust Truth down,
Nor mobs with ropes o'ercome it.

      Tho' cast in prison
Mocked at, jeered, yet Garrison, the great,
Ceased not to plead the cause of the despised slave.
He aroused a nation from its lethargy!
The North viewed with dismay, the horrid beast
The haughty South was nursing in its breast ;
Should this foul thing besmirch Columbia's name?
Should free America, home of the brave,
Become a noissome prison house for slaves!
Not if the trenchant pen or mighty voice
Of Garrison, the noble, could prevent.
By day, by night, in season, out—he passionately
Pleaded for his enslaved countrymen.
So bold a leader could not long lack friends,
Soon honest men became his staunch allies.
The few, became a host! The little stream
Became a flood, resistless, strong, compelling!
      The climax came
In a supreme outburst of blood and carnage,
The strife was fierce, the struggle desperate ;
But, glory be to God, the chains were snapped.
The slaves were freed, and Garrison, immortalized!

      Peace to thy ashes, Honored Dead!
We come today, thy grave to strew with flowers
Of loving words, of honest praise ; we come
Ten million of thy countrymen
Thy bier to consecrate with fragrant incense
Welling up from grateful hearts!

FORAKER AND THE TWENTY-FIFTH.

Who helped Columbia win the day
At San Juan Hill and El Carney,
When brave men faltered in dismay?
     The Twenty-fifth.

Who welcomed then, their timely aid,
Since they to charge were not afraid,
But at the foe like demons made?
     Colonel Roosevelt.

And when the glorious deed was done,
The battles fought and victory won,
Who honor gave to her dark sons?
     The Nation.

Who was it played the scurvy trick,
Who gave the thrust with his Big Stick
That turned bright day to darkness thick?
     Our President.

Where is the place was struck the blow,
The deadly, fatal, unjust blow
Our soldier boys' proud heads bowed low?
     At Brownsville.

Discharged without honor or proof of guilt
Was this the goal toward which they'd built,
The end for which their blood they'd spilt?
     O, mighty God!

Charged with honor up San Juan Hill:
Discharged without honor at dread Brownsville,
Achieved so grandly—rewarded so ill,
     These patriots.

And did no voice for justice cry,
None dare assail the powers high
That did the grievous wrong—none? Ay,
        Brave Foraker.

Alone he braved the mighty wrath,
Alone he dared the lightning's path;
Ha! braver champion no man hath
        Than Foraker.

Defied alone the soldiers' foes,
Himself bared to the cowards' blows;
The price so nobly paid God knows—
        And Foraker.

He suffered in a righteous cause,
Fought to uphold his country's laws,
And won just men's thund'rous applause.
        Great Foraker.

Wherever black men's hearts beat high
For justice, honor, liberty,
Nor name nor deed shall ever die,
        Of gallant J. B. Foraker.

And if a race's steadfast love
A race's loyalty can prove,
No other name is loved above
        The name of Foraker.

ALL HAIL! YE COLORED GRADUATES.

Tune—"All Hail the Power of Jesus' Name."
All hail, ye colored graduates
  From college and from school;
May high ideals each life inspire
  And *service* be its rule!

Let ev'ry citizen and friend
  In our loved country wide,
Join in our hearty song of praise
  And share our righteous pride.

We bid you go as champions brave
  To fight for God and right;
And bring to those who are oppressed
  Great Freedom's glorious light.

You'll find the fields for harvest ripe,
  But laborers very few;
Then forth with willing hearts and strong
  The evil to subdue.

Discouragements will oft confront
  And seek to vanquish you;
But know that naught on earth can thwart
  The man who WILLS to do.

Then forward, onward, upward go!
  And as you boldly press
Your way to life's exalted heights
  The Lord of Hosts will bless.

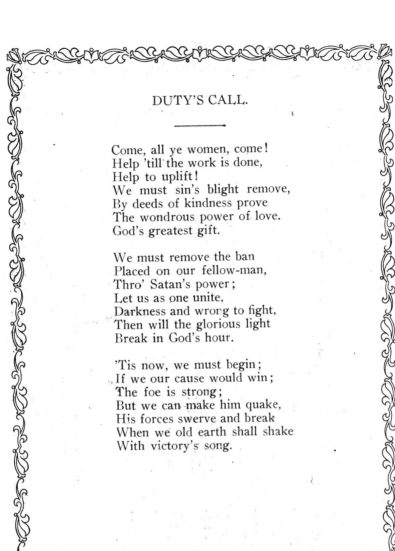

DUTY'S CALL.

Come, all ye women, come!
Help 'till the work is done,
Help to uplift!
We must sin's blight remove,
By deeds of kindness prove
The wondrous power of love.
God's greatest gift.

We must remove the ban
Placed on our fellow-man,
Thro' Satan's power;
Let us as one unite,
Darkness and wrong to fight,
Then will the glorious light
Break in God's hour.

'Tis now, we must begin;
If we our cause would win;
The foe is strong;
But we can make him quake,
His forces swerve and break
When we old earth shall shake
With victory's song.

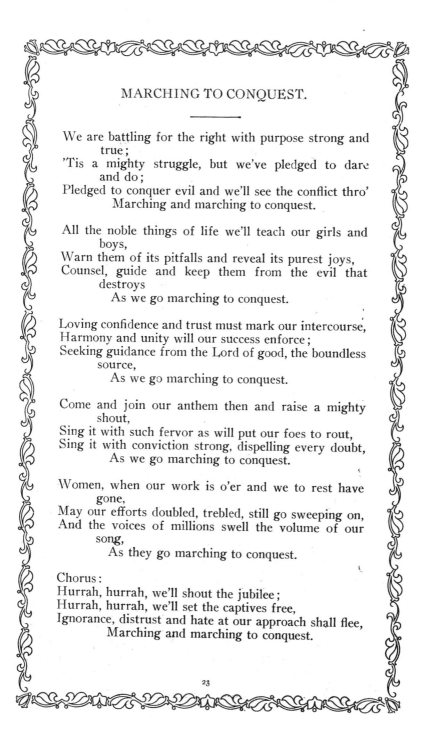# MARCHING TO CONQUEST.

We are battling for the right with purpose strong and
  true;
'Tis a mighty struggle, but we've pledged to dare
  and do;
Pledged to conquer evil and we'll see the conflict thro'
  Marching and marching to conquest.

All the noble things of life we'll teach our girls and
  boys,
Warn them of its pitfalls and reveal its purest joys,
Counsel, guide and keep them from the evil that
  destroys
    As we go marching to conquest.

Loving confidence and trust must mark our intercourse,
Harmony and unity will our success enforce;
Seeking guidance from the Lord of good, the boundless
  source,
    As we go marching to conquest.

Come and join our anthem then and raise a mighty
  shout,
Sing it with such fervor as will put our foes to rout,
Sing it with conviction strong, dispelling every doubt,
    As we go marching to conquest.

Women, when our work is o'er and we to rest have
  gone,
May our efforts doubled, trebled, still go sweeping on,
And the voices of millions swell the volume of our
  song,
    As they go marching to conquest.

Chorus:
Hurrah, hurrah, we'll shout the jubilee;
Hurrah, hurrah, we'll set the captives free,
Ignorance, distrust and hate at our approach shall flee,
    Marching and marching to conquest.

MY BABY.

(On Reading "Souls of Black Folk.")

Who loves my baby? Ah, who loves him not,
  My beautiful baby, who lies fast asleep;
His dimpled brown limbs softly press his white cot,
  And angels, God's messengers, guard o'er him keep.

Who hates my baby? Ah, merciful God,
  Thy children—his brothers whose faces are white;
"Black skin is a crime: pass thou under the rod,"
  They cry! "This is our country, and might makes us
    right."

My baby! immortal soul, dark tho' he be;
  Where shall I take him for safety and peace,
Where in this land of the brave and the free
  Shall baby and I find of terror surcease?

Justice, I ask for my baby is all,
  And freedom to grow and expand all his powers;
Then right give the verdict—to stand or to fall—
  While Hatred of Race before Righteousness cowers.

Then, if my dark baby, unworthy be found,
  Incompetent, lustful, unfaithful or base,
I'll abide by the verdict and utter no sound
  Agree that beneath is my dark baby's place.

But glory to God! who my dark baby gave
  A mind, soul and being like unto his own
And sent his dear son my brown baby to save
  From the seeds of corruption the Tempter has sown.

Right my baby will place side by side with your child,
  And Right will erase from your heart that fierce hate;
Will you bide by the verdict of Right? Will the wild
  And ignoble prejudice die e'er too late?

For be thou assured, God's bright angels will guard
  My baby so brown, to the heavenly portal,
White soul, not white face, shall there gain its reward,
  For Right keeps the gate to the City Immortal.

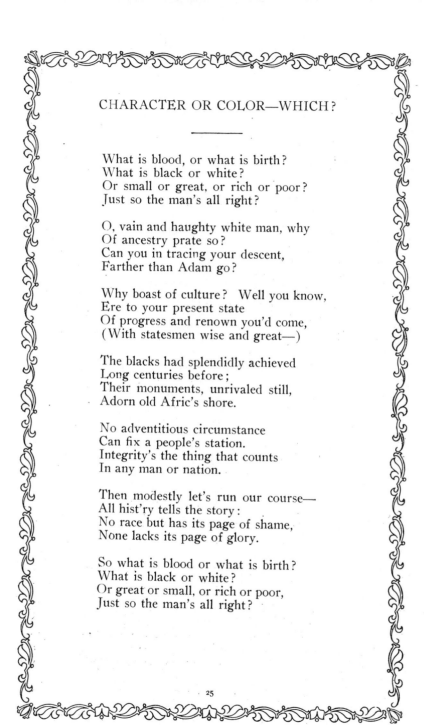

CHARACTER OR COLOR—WHICH?

What is blood, or what is birth?
What is black or white?
Or small or great, or rich or poor?
Just so the man's all right?

O, vain and haughty white man, why
Of ancestry prate so?
Can you in tracing your descent,
Farther than Adam go?

Why boast of culture? Well you know,
Ere to your present state
Of progress and renown you'd come,
(With statesmen wise and great—)

The blacks had splendidly achieved
Long centuries before;
Their monuments, unrivaled still,
Adorn old Afric's shore.

No adventitious circumstance
Can fix a people's station.
Integrity's the thing that counts
In any man or nation.

Then modestly let's run our course—
All hist'ry tells the story:
No race but has its page of shame,
None lacks its page of glory.

So what is blood or what is birth?
What is black or white?
Or great or small, or rich or poor,
Just so the man's all right?

THE DREAMER.

"The Dreamers are the Saviours of the World."
So ran the legend writ in letters bold,
Upon a page whereon in idle hour,
My listless gaze did chance to rest. Straightway
A magic thrill thro' all my being ran
And all my powers of mind became at once
Instinct with leaping life. Again I gazed—
Again with eagerness the page I scanned:
Unchanged, the words still boldly graven there
"The Dreamers are the Saviours of the World."
"And can it be," I thought, this ancient page
Doth to my own sweet wild imaginings
Lend confirmation strong. Would this bright world
Be but a barren waste, a wilderness;
Its human creatures scarcely one remove
From birds and beasts, and creeping, crawling things
Instead of beings, as great God declared
But little lower than the angels formed,
Did not the Dreamer—Sculptor, Poet, Sage—
Keep ever brightly burning life's ideals
As beacon lights to comfort, cheer and guide
The weary travelers o'er life's rugged way?
Still motionless I sat, still pondered o'er
The words this ancient tome did speak, dramatic
And profound, as 'twere an oracle.
The book, unheeded, fell from my lax hand,
And back with lightning speed my fancy flew
O'er space and time immense and limitless.
Before mine eyes a panorama spread,
Showing the great of earth since time began.
I saw bold Caesar and Napoleon,
St. Francis of Assisi, Socrates,
Shakespeare and Froebel, Michael Angelo
And all the sacred host of mighty dead.
Before me moved the pageant of the years
In ghostly pomp and grandeur. I saw again
The youthful Joseph, Dreamer of Israel;
Despised of his brethren, cursed and roughly used
Because he dreamed the truth they could not grasp.
And then, I saw the dream fulfilled, while they,

The former scoffers, bent the suppliant knee,
In silent tribute to the Dreamer's power.
When busy Martha cumbered with much care
Complained that Mary at the Saviour's feet
In dreamland sat, the gentle Christ replied,
"Mary hath chosen the better part." I saw
Columbus, bold and unafraid, set out
Upon an unknown sea his dream to find
Come true. Douglass, the slave—the martyr, Brown,
And Harriet Beecher Stowe, the prophetess,
Each dreaming of a country free from rule
Of grasping greed and heartless tyranny,
In patience wrought, to bring to pass the dream
Which men derided—called impossible:
When lo! while yet they mocked, it came to pass!
"Dreamers," I thought, whose dreams have changed
        the world!
So must it ever be. The Dreamer comes
In every age unvalued and condemned.
The Doers trooping come, with boisterous haste
Millions to one lone Dreamer: failing him,
No single revolution of the wheel
Of progress marks advance, for he alone
Can move the world and bring a revelation.
The true Idealist does not spend his time
In vain and idle musings; nor does he flee
Unfavorable conditions, as a slave,
For quarters more secure and genial:
But rather, he is one who patiently
And often painfully his life doth shape
Harmonious with an inward purpose true,
Striving against cold materialism to make
The glorious vision in whose light he lives
Shine strong and bright before the eyes of men
Whose sight less clear discerning is than his.
'Tis true that dreams are but the evidence
Of things unseen—realities which all
Shall one day see and know. Dream lofty dreams,
And as you dream, O, Friend, shall you become
What you desire, you shall obtain; and what
You shall aspire unto you shall achieve.
Your vision is the promise of what you
Shall one day be; your ideal but the prophecy
Of what you shall at last unveil!
Then cherish well your vision, cherish fondly
Your ideals, O great and noble Dreamer!

WE'LL DIE FOR LIBERTY.

We are children of oppression who are struggling to
    be free
From injustice, and the galling yoke of color-tyranny;
Our small band is facing bravely a relentless enemy.
        But we go fighting on.

For liberty we'll bare our breasts, and this our cry
    shall be:
"Equal rights and equal justice, equal opportunity,"
Undaunted we will face the foe and fight right valiantly
        To victory marching on.

In the name of Christ our Lord who suffered death
    upon the tree,
And of the Constitution, our proud country's guarantee,
And of the flag which over all should wave protectingly
        We'll strike for liberty.

Thus strongly fortified in right we'll strive triumph-
    antly,
Till the glorious light of Freedom's torch shall flame
    from sea to sea;
And all the children of our land shall dwell in amity,
        As Truth goes marching on.

Then list, ye Sons of Morning, to a weaker brother's
    plea,
And harken, Hosts of Darkness, to our Heaven-
    inspired decree:
As He died to make men holy we will die for liberty,
        Thou, God, the issue keep.

      Chorus: Glory, glory, hallelujah! ||
      We'll die for liberty!
        || Repeat three times.

THE WIDENING LIGHT

THE WIDENING LIGHT

BY

CARRIE WILLIAMS CLIFFORD

WALTER REID COMPANY

BOSTON

CONDÉ NAST PRESS   GREENWICH, CONN.

To

MY RACE

CONTENTS

THE WIDENING LIGHT

("*But above all comes the New Spirit.*" CRISIS.)

A sound of muttering, faint and far and low—
A sound of stirring restlessly about—
A harsher note and frequently a shout—
Of red defiance? not of peace I trow;
Oh, self deceived and blind who do not know
The meaning of this unaccustomed rout!
Do you not feel the frenzy? Can you doubt
The triumph of Race Hatred's overthrow?
The moving millions of the darker clan
Have wakened to Jehovah's ancient cry—
Not stunted, greedy, boastful, pale-faced man
Omnipotent is—"verily none save I!"
And piercing the dark clouds of dreadful night
Behold! they greet the light, the light, The Light!

[ix]

A TOAST TO AFRICA

Christmas, 1920

From a goblet of rarest and richest red gold,
Encrusted with jewels of value untold,
All flowing and glowing with nectar of wine,
Distilled from the spirits of souls sweet and fine
As these sons and daughters whose deeds I rehearse,
With zeal all-consuming, though halting my verse—
I drink to my Race on this epochal morn,
Remembering the Christ-child who came lowly-
    born,—
Was despised, crucified and rejected of men,
But *now* to whom honor and glory—Amen!

MOTHERS OF AMERICA

A sonnet celebrating the heroism and valor of the women
of America, black and white, in the Great War
for world democracy, 1917–1918

Ye, Queen, who bear the birth-pangs of a world,
To whom the nations in this hour of stress,
For succor look, and for the ruth to bless,
Ye, great, whose fondled darlings, combed and curled,
Are in the shell-torn, foreign trenches hurled,
To stay the hellish Hun, who else would press,
The cup of degradation and distress,
To lips of men with freedom's flag unfurled—
Ye valiant mother-band who gladly gave,
The first-fruits of your riven wombs to save,
The world from horrors darker than the grave,
Ye are the Brave, who in your country's need
Did sow the trenches with your Precious Seed—
The greatest gift of war, and valor's noblest deed.

TO PHYLLIS WHEATLEY

(First African Poetess)

No! Not like the lark, didst thou circle and sing,
High in the heavens on morn's merry wing,
But hid in the depths of the forest's dense shade,
There where the homes of the lowly were made,
Thou nested! Though fettered, thou frail child of night,
Thy melody trilled forth with naive delight;
And all through the throes of the night dark and long,
Earth's favored ones harkened thy ravishing song,
So plaintive and wild, touched with Africa's lilt;
Of wrong small complaint, sweet forgiveness of guilt —
Oh, a lyric of love and a paean of praise,
Didst thou at thy vespers, Dark Nightingale, raise;
So sweet was the hymn rippling out of the dark,
It rivalled the clear morning song of the lark.

[3]

FREDERICK DOUGLASS

(In honor of the centenary of his birth—February 1817-1917)

A century of mighty thoughts has passed,
Of mighty deeds and Merlin-magic years,
Since first his infant wail assailed the ears
That knew not how prophetic was the blast!
Then swiftly sped the years into the vast
Store-house of time! The bitter vale-of-tears
Was vanquished, and the dark abyss-of-fears;
The thing, transformed, became a *Soul* at last!
Search noble history's most stirring page,
And tell what life excelled his in the race;
Trace deeds of daring men in every age
And say if one out-rivalled this dark face.
Great Douglass—*slave* and *fugitive* and *Man*,
With the immortal host, thou art in the van!

[4]

WILLIAM STANLEY BRAITHWAITE

(*To William Stanley Braithwaite upon his visit to Washington, D. C., April, 1916*)

An Appreciation

He came like John of old to all proclaiming
The Bread of Life; to our starved senses bringing
The breath of April in his offerings!
The resurrection of our better selves
Commanded he: the spirit-half of our
Dual existence, called he back to life;
Revived in us the ancient thirst for Truth,
The search for Beauty 'long the dusty ways
And sordid places of our journeyings.
Like John he came to our world-wilderness
The real from the false to separate;
The Light to set before our stumbling feet!
And some whose ears had long been deaf to Truth,
Whose hearts thro' greed had hardened into stones,
Were purified, revived and lifted up
By the persuasive magic of his song.

L'Envoi

O poet, with thy soul-wrought visionings,
O prophet, with thy wise philosophies,
O poet-prophet, prophet-poet, Come
Again to our low dwelling-places! Come

[5]

And bring the balm of healing on thy tongue!
Oh, wash us clean with fresh Aprilian showers,
Re-light the altar candles of our souls!

[6]

TO HOWARD UNIVERSITY

(Semi-Centennial Celebration, March, 1917)

The pall of battle scarce had passed away,
Hearts yet were hot with hate and hard with greed,
When some love-kindled spirit hid the seed,
Whose spreading branches shelter us today;
Beloved Mother, you for whom we pray,
Be fortified to meet our every need,
At your full breasts the hungry children feed,
Nor turn a single thirsting soul away!
What hath God wrought in fifty years! we've crossed
The Valley-of-Humiliation: then
Advancing up the Hill-of-Progress, tossed
A Challenge to the world of other men.
And reaching out for all that's manhood's due
Our thanks go winging up to God—and *You!*

[7]

PAUL LAURENCE DUNBAR

(*Upon reading the Introduction to "Lyrics of Lowly Life"*
by William Dean Howells)

The beetling night was fading toward the dawn,
When strange, weird sounds smote subtly on the ear
Of one far up the heights, who paused to hear
The song of him, who doggedly pressed on
From that low vale whence Hope seemed almost gone.
Persistently the sound rose loud and clear
Surcharged of times with radiating cheer—
Of times with sadness of a soul in pawn.

The hearthside lyrics trickled from his heart,
With simple melody and baffling art!
A traveller above called down the slope
And Dunbar answered, "*Comrade!* now I hope!"
One white, one black, but *one in spirit*, they
Symbolic are of God's Eternal Way!

[8]

WITHIN THE VEIL

And ye, who view life darkly thro' a veil
At length shall read its riddle face to face!
The hidden springs of beauty and the grace
Of fuller living, wait beyond this trail
Blood-stained and steep: there stands the Holy Grail
Whose healing waters shall the woes efface,
Of plodding pilgrims, who still seek the place
Where men of every race shall say, "All hail!"
To this broad shrine, we too shall bring our gift
Of joyous laughter, song and loyal love;
And rank on rank still surging up, we'll lift
Hosannahs to the God-of-Worlds, above!
His listening ear will catch our minor, sweet,
Making the concord of the spheres complete!

[9]

A DREAM OF DEMOCRACY

Depressed in spirit and harassed by thought
Of war, and all its festering, foul brood,—
Grim death, gaunt suffering and loathsome food—
I fell into a trance, being much o'er-wrought:
A vision marvelous my fancy caught!
Afar upon the Mount of Ages, stood
Old Father Time; and from his hands a flood—
(Increased by countless putrid streams that brought
Debris of all earth's cruelty and crime,
Intolerance, injustice, rape and wrong,
Until the putrefaction, stench and slime
Befouled the universe)—*swept swift along*,
And lost itself in a deep crystal sea,—
The cleansing Ocean of Democracy.

PERIL

As, when some filthy sore grows menacing,
Polluting all the currents of pure air,
Dispersing its vile atoms everywhere—
While with death-poisoned tentacles they cling,
To our hearts' treasuries, devouring,
And laying waste the temples of our care,—
The surgeon with blade kind but firm lays bare
And cuts away the flesh, foul, festering:—
So must the learned doctors of the State
Relentlessly cut the leprous sore
Of prejudice! else will they find too late,
Its rank corruption eating thro' the core
Of human brotherhood! Grim germs of Hate,
Razing our kingdom with titanic roar!

SOUL-GROWTH

(Upon the lack of opportunity afforded the Negro)

Atom of God! spark of the Infinite!
Illimitable thy majestic sway,
Where influences salutary play,
Thy powers to unfold to utmost height!
Potential gods, all, all who strive aright,
Defended from the pompous world's array
Of hostile forces, dragging to decay
Ideals of highest honor, truth and right:
Nurtured by rain and shine the queenly rose
In sheltered garden to perfection grows;
But on the desert, without loving care,
Is left to perish miserably there.
So with the Soul! if faith and culture fail,
"'Twill grow deformed and choked within the veil"!

NEGRO PLAYERS ON BROADWAY

*(The Ridgley Torrence plays presented on Broadway
by Mrs. Emilie G. Hapgood, April, 1917)*

Behold! a Star is trembling in the East,
Whose pale light heralds a triumphant day,
The greatness of whose promise none can say,
Nor who the guest of honor at the feast,
When from the thrall of prejudice released,
Men see the Soul behind the Veil of Clay.
Then brother recognizing brother, may
Divine that least is great and great is least.

A beacon in the wilderness, O Star,
With ox-like eyes we note your lureful gleam.
And Star, so faintly shining from afar,
With God-like faith we watch the widening stream
Of light!   Ho, Christ has come! the perfect day
In glory breaks never to pass away!

[13]

THE GOAL

("To make the world safe for democracy")

Exalted goal! Oh, coveted ideal,
Which but to contemplate, causes to steal
Within the heart, the sting of ecstasy!
Oh, fateful words! Oh, potent prophecy,
Which yet shall make entrenched wrong to reel
And stagger from the place of power—to feel
The odium of men, outraged, set free!
Tho' *now* the words are empty, void of life,
And soothly uttered to allay the strife
And discontent with which the world is rife,
These words shall yet become a fervent creed,
And vivified to meet The Peoples' need,
Shall fructify into heroic deed.

RACE-HATE

(On the East St. Louis riot, July 28, 1917)

What infamies have been condoned, O Hate,
What sin, what guilt, what horrors in thy name!
Such bestial revelries which else would shame
The darkest heathen in his virgin state!
Yet know that judgment on thine acts doth wait,
And Time will write with pen of leaping flame
The ghastly story—how thou didst defame
God's living temples—craven, crafty Hate!
For thou hast none deceived, not e'en thyself,
Thy bloody hands are raised for power and pelf!
Hath not the lesson of the Ages taught,
Thy seeming triumphs are too dearly bought?
Cold seas of blood convulse thy coward heart;
Already crushed, defeated, doomed thou art!

[15]

SILENT PROTEST PARADE

(On Fifth Avenue, New York, Saturday, July 28, 1917,
protesting against the St. Louis riots)

Were you there? Did you see? Gods! wasn't it fine!
Did you notice how straight we kept the line,
As we marched down the famous avenue,
Silent, dogged and dusky of hue,
Keeping step to the sound of the muffled drum,
With its constantly recurring *tum—tum, tum—*
Tum—Tum—Tum—Tum—Tum;
Ten thousand of us, if there was one!
As goodly a sight as this ancient sun
Has ever looked upon!

                        Youth and maid
Father, mother—not one afraid
Or ashamed to let the whole world know
What he thought of the hellish East St. Louis "show,"
Orgy—riot—mob—what you will,
Where men and e'en women struggled to kill
Poor black workers, who'd fled in distress from the South
To find themselves murdered and mobbed in the North.

We marched as a protest—we carried our banner,
On which had been boldly inscribed every manner
Of sentiment—all, to be sure, within reason—
But no flag—not that we meant any treason—
Only who'd have the heart to carry Old Glory,

[16]

After hearing all of the horrible story,
Of East St. Louis? and never a word,
From the nation's head, as if he'd not heard
The groans of the dying ones here at home,
Though 'tis plain he can hear even farther than Rome.

Oh, yes, I was there in the Silent Parade,
And a man (he was white) I heard when he said,
"If they had music now, 'twould be great!"—
"We march not, sir, with hearts elate,
But sad; we grieve for our dark brothers
Murdered, and we hope that others
Will heed our protest against wrong,
Will help to make our protest strong."

Were you there? Ah, brothers, wasn't it fine!
The children—God bless 'em—headed the line;
Then came the mothers dressed in white,
And some—my word! 'twas a thrilling sight—
Carried their babies upon their breast,
Face tense and eager as forward they pressed,
With never a laugh and never a word,
But ever and always, the thing they heard
Was the *tum—tum—, tum, tum,*
Of the muffled drum—*tum, tum, tum!*

And last the black-coated men swung by,
Head up, chest firm, determined eye—
I was so happy, I wanted to cry.

[17]

As I watched the long lines striding by,
(Ten thousand souls if there was one)
And I knew that "to turn, the worm had begun,"
As we marched down Fifth Avenue unafraid
And calm, in our first Silent Protest Parade!

LITTLE MOTHER

(Upon the lynching of Mary Turner)

Oh, tremble, Little Mother,
For your dark-eyed, unborn babe,
Whom in your secret heart you've named
The well-loved name of "Gabe."

    For Gabriel is the father's name,
    And the son is sure to be
    "Just like his father!" as she wants
    The whole, wide world to see!

But tremble, Little Mother,
For your unborn baby's fate;
The father tarries long away—
Why does he stay so late?

    For dark the night and weird the wind,
    And chilled the heart with fear!
    What are those hideous sounds and cries
    Each instant drawing near?

Oh, tremble, dark-faced mother,
At the dreadful word that falls
From lips of pale-faced demons,
As the black man pleads and calls.

    For they're dragging Gabe, at a stout rope's end,
    And they say, "She is bound to tell!"

[19]

Something she knows not a thing about,
Or they'll "Give her the same as well!"

Oh, tremble, helpless mother!
They're beating down the door,
And you'll never feel the father's kiss,
Or the stir of the baby more.

Oh, the human beasts were ruthless,
And there upon the ground,
Two bodies—and an unborn babe—
The ghastly morning found.

DECEIVED

To war I gave my first-born, debonair
And over-flowing with the joy of life!
His heart was empty of all thought of strife—
He dreamed of radiant life devoid of care.

When next Columbia called I gave—I gave—
My little lad, my babe, my youngest-born,
Full of the light and promise of the morn,
And ready his beloved land to save.

These two I gave, my first-born and my last,
The Alpha and Omega of my love's dream,
So rudely shattered by war's lurid gleam—
My all into her seething cauldron cast!

Whose—whose the condemnation then, if I
Shame the false lips that lured them with a lie?

THE BLACK DRAFTEE FROM DIXIE

*(Twelve Negro soldiers who had served overseas were
lynched upon their return to their homes in the South)*

Upon his dull ear fell the stern command;
And tho' scarce knowing why or whither, he
Went forth prepared to battle loyally,
And questioned not your faith, O Dixie-land!

And tho' the task assigned were small or grand,—
If toiling at mean tasks ingloriously,
Or in fierce combat fighting valiantly,—
With poise magnificent he took his stand!

What tho' the hero-warrior was black?
His heart was white and loyal to the core;
And when to his loved Dixie he came back,
Maimed, in the duty done on foreign shore,
Where from the hell of war he never flinched,
Because he cried, "*Democracy*," was lynched.

TERCENTENARY
OF THE LANDING OF SLAVES AT JAMESTOWN

1619-1919

Upon the slaver's deck, a motley band
Of blacks looked out upon the boundless main,
Knowing with anguished hearts that ne'er again
Their feet, with pride, would press their native land;
Theirs thenceforth to obey the rude command
Of masters, wielding cruel lash and chain,
Wringing three centuries of toil and pain
From helpless slaves!—Then waved war's magic wand,
And, at the sign, up rose twelve million men—
A brave, patriotic host, of great power,
To serve America in her crucial hour:
Titanic power, to bless or curse; for when
Pent wrong, injustice and oppression break,
Vesuvius-like, the heart of earth they shake!

[23]

TOMORROW

("*Ethiopia shall stretch forth her hand*")

Tomorrow! magic word of promise rare,
What witchery inheres in thy sweet name,
Inspiring wild ambition, naught can tame,
To conquer failure—here or otherwhere;
The rosy rapture thou dost ever bear
Upon thy brow, is but the beacon-flame—
The luminous lodestone, luring on to fame
And high endeavor! Simple friend, beware
The fool who says, "Tomorrow—never comes";
For opportunities like bursting bombs
Shall blast the walls that limit us Today.
And *all*, who wish within *its* scope to stay.
Time has no end save in eternity
Of which *Tomorrow* is the prophecy.

[24]

FUTILITY

(To be a Negro in America!)

To feel emotion struggling and to need
O Christ, the power to speak the pregnant word,
That o'er these earthly thunders might be heard
And flame the souls of men to glorious deed—

To know the spirit's urge to rise and lead
The "hosts that sit in darkness"—to be stirred
To light a world, by wrong dimmed and blurred,
To cry aloud against the groveling greed
Of men, with faces ominous and pale,
Who stultify the souls of darker men,—
All this to see, to know, to feel and then—
And then, ignoble, shameful word, to *fail*,
Because convention spurns my human cry,
Because, oh, luckless fortune, *I am I!*

OUR WOMEN OF THE CANTEEN

Who shall tell the story of our women of the canteen?
Our women, golden, dusk and brown
Ministering in France to our brave boys,
Our brave, black boys
Fighting in Flanders!
Our stevedores in France unloading the ships,
Building the roads in Picardy,
That world-democracy might be a dream come true!
Was a soldier broken, dazed and exhausted by the hell
    of war?
Was his heart breaking with thoughts of home?
Did he yearn hungrily for mother, wife or sister?

Then would come these women
Dusk and gold and brown,
And with the tender, ministering hand of mother,
Or with the camaraderie of sister
Or the soul-sympathy of an understanding wife,
These dark women of the canteen
Would mirror to our boys
A bit of home, in France,
Heartening them for a return to the trenches,
And to the building of the roads,
And the unloading of the ships.
Oh, who shall sing the glory
Of our women of the canteen!

[26]

THE FREEDMAN

Agéd and broken and helpless,
Sapped with the toil of years,
Dumbly he questions the future,
Haunted and shaken with fears.

Slowly he searches the sad past;
Naught does he find there to shame
Faith of his heart—*he* was loyal,
But *whose* was the treason—the blame?

Blindly he faces Life's problems;
Where are his children? full five
Filial sons strove and labored;
He knows not if *one* be alive!

Meekly he ponders, he wonders,
Why, in God's name, he should be
Adrift without rudder or compass,
Sore-smitten with age, on Life's sea.

Vainly he questions the Power
Almighty, that sweeps us along,
The lonely ones sighing and crying,
The mighty rejoicing with song.

Agéd and broken and helpless,
Sapped with the toil of the years,
Dumbly he questions the future
Haunted and shaken with fears.

[27]

AN EASTER MESSAGE

Now quivering to life, all nature thrills
At the approach of that triumphant queen,
Pink-fingered Easter, trailing robes of green
Swishingly o'er the flower-embroidered hills,
Her hair perfumed of myriad daffodils:
Upon her trembling bosom now is seen
The frail sweet lilies with their snowy sheen
As sprightly she o'ersteps the springtime rills.
To black folk choked within the deadly grasp
Of racial hate, what message does she bring
Of resurrection and the hope of spring?
Assurance their death-stupor is a mask—
A sleep, with elements potential rife,
Ready to burst full-flowered into life!

SHRINES

Each heart bows low before some cherished shrine!—
Westminster Abbey with its sainted dead
Is hallowed ground where millions yet shall tread;
Love rears the Taj Mahal of rare design,
And wondrous beauty wrought in every line;
To Rome and Athens other hosts have led,
And where the great Napoleon makes his bed;
The faithful dream of ancient Palestine.
Some seek the home of poet, martyr, seer,
Of ruler, beggar, saint or cavalier,
According as these lives have left impress
Upon the soul of man, his life to bless.
Each heart bows low before some cherished shrine—
The bitter cross where John Brown hung is *mine*.

LIKE YOU

Like you, He came unknown and poor,
And closed to Him was every door.

His race, like yours, was held in scorn,
Like yours, was humble and forlorn.

Like you, He was of men despised!
(So deeply was the King disguised.)

The Roman rulers heeded not
The manger-cradle,—His rude cot.

But Wise Men watching in the East
Knew, the *greatest* is often *least*.

They followed His Star, brought priceless things,
Bowed low and worshipped the King of Kings!

[30]

THREE SONNETS

I

Appeal

Three centuries beneath your haughty heel,
Humble and ignorant, debased and poor,
Like mendicants before your Temple-door,
The potentates of earth have seen us kneel.
With guileless art we made our mute appeal,
And tho' you scorned and spurned us, tried the more
To love and serve you better than before.
Your children we have nursed, your evening meal
Set forth: your crops have reaped, your acres tilled,
Your burdens borne, your enemies have killed;
We've given of our brawn unstintingly,
And of our brain, when so you'd let it be.
Remembering all, how can you lynch and hate,
And with our quivering clay, your passion sate?

II

Demand

Torn from our heritage against our will,
And here detained by blood-hound and by lash,
From dawn to darkness driven by "po' white trash,"
The onerous tasks to do,—the soil to till,
Helping your dream of empire to fulfill—
Thro' blood-baptism and the clanging clash

[31]

Of war, and its swift clarifying flash—
The present finds us citizens (tho' *nil*
Our rights and powers in the common state)—
Who with the volume of Niagara's roar
And strength with which her giant waters pour,
Demand, with vigor which shall not abate
All the prerogatives which are our due
Without regard to race or creed or hue.

III

WARNING

The Law that spins these toy-top worlds in space,
Divides the opaque darkness from the day,
Directs the shining of each solar ray,
Guides and controls the stellar chariot-race,
And holds the whirling universe in place—
Altho' no particle may stop or stay—
This Law immutable, you may not sway,
Or modify, or alter by your grace!
Unfailingly the tides of ocean flow,
The giant oaks and modest pansies grow,
Inexorably following the deed
Comes without haste and without pause, the meed.
A tiny tendril creviced in the rock,
In time will burst apart a granite block.

[32]

OLD IRONSIDES!

*(Formerly the estate of Commodore Stewart, commander of vessel
of the same name, and famous in the Civil War; now a
school for the training of Colored Youth)*

Old Ironsides! Historic spot so fair,
Whose generous-spreading acres beckon, where
In silent beauty sweeps the Delaware,
I love you!

High on your bluff commanding
I looked afar,
And saw in retrospect the place where war
Dark, grim and terrible
Forced Washington and his brave men
Barefoot across the icy flood,
Fighting for independence!
'Twas liberty for which they fought—
Relief from tyranny they sought—
These heroes whom I sing.

Around this hallowed spot there cling,
E'en yet soul-stirring memories,
Of those who walked your paths!
Have not these groves re-echoed to the cry
"Before we bend to tyrants, we will die!"
Brave souls who wrought ofttimes perchance in pain,
Yet not one agony endured in vain!

Time has destroyed "The Mansion" utterly,

[33]

And here the walk has crumbled to decay;
Upon that knoll, rank grows the shrubbery,
And if one glances yonder, there one sees
The avenue of old wild-cherry trees—
Dim vestiges of former glory!
Now gone are those who labored, hoped and loved;
Yet their indomitable spirit lives,
And to these dark-faced children gives
The moving inspiration!

Today I note your busy crowded halls,
Filled with those youths whom learning calls
To higher destinies!
The noisy workshop sounds again
To tune of hammer, saw and plane,
As earnest effort moulds to shape
The useful things that go to make
Man's lot more comfortable.

If to be striving—contented in the work,—
Which none would think to shirk,—
If to love nature and her beauties rare,
Here bountifully spread with careless care,
If to be drinking at the fount
Which makes men wise,
And all-encircling the cerulean skies—
If these things make the heaven for which man sighs,
Then here, Old Ironsides, is paradise!

[34]

THE FLIGHT

Away down south in Dixie-land
The place where they were born,
Where grows the cotton, silver-white
Tobacco, cane and corn—

I see your beauty, feel your charm;
I knew your ancient lure
For those dark earth-sprites, who for you
Did pain untold endure!

But now the cabin lonely stands
Beneath the spreading tree;
The old plantation echoes not
The weird slave-melody!

Gone! all are gone! how strange it seems!
I miss their gleaming eyes—
Their loud guffaws, whose hearty ring
Floats lightly to the skies.

What do they seek? Where have they fled?
Why do they roam afar?
They go to find the Promised Land,
With gates of Hope ajar.

Where schools stand ready to impart
The precious Rule of Three;

[35]

And high ambition may be served
To even the last degree.

Where aspiration soars aloft,
And self-respect may grow;
Where none would limit nor confine
The man who wants *to know*.

O Southland, that they loved so well,
The time will come when you
Wishing them back, will learn the truth
That faithful friends are few!

WEEDS

The little house in which I live looks out
Upon a garden, where I love to walk,
Or sit and dream and listen to the talk
Of others, moving restlessly about.
Sometimes the echo of a merry shout,—
Again the raucous tones of those who mock,
Of those who yield and e'en of those who knock,
Inflame my heart, or chill my soul with doubt.

These human plants within the garden growing
Are they the fruit, the sample of the sowing?
And the stink-weeds that flourish wildly there,
Are they as well the objects of His care?
Of malice, envy, hate and strife, God knows
Injustice is the rankest weed that grows.

THE GIFT

A priceless gift within your hand is laid,
A jewel fashioned by the Master's art;
No fleck or flaw bedims its perfect heart,
More precious than are emeralds—opals—jade.
This gift, for which gold never can be paid,
Is freely given by a Friend, whose part
It is to teach its magic—to impart
A knowledge of the *why* the gift was made.
Possession of this talismanic gift,
Like old Aladdin's wonder-lamp, will lift
Earth mortals high as heaven, rightly used;
But doom to Stygian darkness, if abused.
'Tis yours to will what picture shall appear:
The gift, a pure, unsullied, glad New Year!

[38]

RESPITE

At close of day, I couch me at my ease
In solitude, far from dull mammon's roar,
And let the rain of thought upon me pour
In showers, hard or soft as they may please:
Sometimes like gentle patter, thro' the trees,
Of joyous rains of spring, they touch the core
Of my parched self, reviving flowers of yore—
Pansies and sweet forget-me-nots, to tease
Old memories! sometimes a torrent breaks
Raging with fiendish fury 'til it shakes
My world of dreams wrecking my castles there,
Leaving my gardens desolate and bare,
When, from life's gilded pleasures shut away,
I seek my lonely couch at close of day.

[39]

THE BIRTH OF A NATION

Stay! vain, deluded man!
Know not you never can
Attain unto your high estate and rich,
While holding your dark brother in the ditch?

Hold! rash, misguided fool!
Why will you be the tool
Of passions, devilish, ignoble, base,
Wherein no God-like action one can trace?

Traducer of a race,
You, who are fair of face,
Stop! lest the children of a darker hue
In love, shall prove superior to you!

O, brother, pause! reflect!
Each cause has its effect,
This is the law: your acts or soon or late,
Will reap a bounteous harvest,—hate for hate.

PRAYER FOR DELIVERANCE

Father omnipotent,
God of the universe,
Thou Great Jehovah,
    We humbly beseech Thee!

Harken our loud lament,
See Thou our naked need,
Heed Thou our earnest prayer,
    Witness our tears!

Father, the enemy
Stealeth our lives away,
Feedeth us bitter bread,
    Abaseth our pride!

O God of Abraham,
Isaac and Jacob,
Of saints and of prophets,
    Our trust is in Thee!

Scourge him who scoffeth us—
Useth us despitefully—
Stealeth our substance—
    Thy vengeance, we pray!

O Thou who knowest all,
O Thou who seest all,
O Thou who rulest all,
    Flay and spare not!

[41]

VANITAS

He breathlessly pursued the dream of Fame
Spurred on by a desire insatiate,
To win a place secure and make a name
Renowned! Thus daily striving, soon and late
He wrought; but ever as he closer came
The goal receded: then with quickened gait,
Disdaining aught of censure or of blame,
He gained the height he sought with heart elate!
Oh, blessed height which he had seen afar,
Thro' gloom and sunshine, thro' distress and pain,
But ever luring, guiding as the star
Of hope, or as the rainbow after rain:
When lo! the sacred Temple-door was barred
Against his tarnished, craven soul, sin-scarred!

MOODS

Daybreak in the meadow
   and the song of the lark in the sky;
All my hopes are winging and soaring
   —so high, so high!

Nightfall in the forest
   and the nightingale's sobbing song;
All my hopes are dead and the darkness
   —so long, so long!

TO ——

Dear friend of mine whose magnet-heart
Hath joined mine own to thee,
Where'er with changing years thou art
Or near or far from me.

O friend of mine, I'd have thee know
How dear I hold thy worth!
Thy sweet companionship, I vow
O'ertops the gauds of earth.

Dear friend of mine, this faithful thought
May joy and solace be,—
Not separation, death, no! *Naught*
Can change my love for thee!

SON

We wandered through the meadow, green and cool,
My romping, joyous little son and I.
Bright was the rippling stream and we, withal,
So gay, we noted not the flying hours
'Til suddenly the sun had set, and gray,
Dim shadows o'er the earth began to creep.

No longer now he sang in childish glee,
Or sought the modest flower in cranny hid;
But close beside me walked in sober mood,
His hand close-clasped in mine; then coaxingly,
"'Tis dark, dear father; please, sir, take me home!"

My little son to manhood now has grown;
No longer fears he shadows dim and gray;
In fearlessness of youth, he braves the dark,
But I, who know the dangers of the dark
And all the ills which do in darkness lurk,

Am fearful, lest he stumble and so fall
Into the pit: but when Life's Day is done,
When burst all the bubbles he has chased,
And creeping come the shadows of the night,
Do Thou, dear Father, hold his trembling hand
And through the darkness lead him gently Home.

[45]

FRIENDSHIP

Not by the dusty stretch of days
Slow-gathering to lengthening years
 We measure friendship's chain,
But by the understanding touch,
The smile, the soul-kiss, yea, the tears
 That ease the load of pain.

ABANDONMENT

I want to sail out on the flood-tide of life,
To the uttermost reaches of self;
Forgetting the petty conventions of men,
And the scramble for power and pelf.

I want to sail out to the Island-of-Love,
And couch myself there on your breast,
To be soothed by your passionate viol-sweet voice,
And lulled by its music to rest.

I want to be warmed by the sun of your smile,
Refreshed by the rain of your tears,
Content in the clasp of your compassing arms,
As we drift down the tide of the years.

I want to float out on the ebb-tide of life,
As mutely the death watch you keep,
And feel the quick pulse of your quivering lips
As I fall in the last dreamless sleep.

TEARS

The World today is sad,
No light is in her eye,
How cold and pale she seems!
The dull, gray ashes on her lips
Choke back the rippling thrills of glee
That yesterday, a joyous river flowed.
Why does she weep incessantly—
With now and then a momentary lull
Succeeded by an outburst
More terrific?
I wonder if her heart like mine,
Pent and restrained,
Is sometimes full beyond control!
Then comes the torrent, merciful,
Relieving, cleansing, purging,
And washing free of care and dross,
The Soul left clean and purified.

QUEST

My goal out-distances the utmost star,
Yet is encompassed in my inmost Soul;
I *am* my goal—my quest, to know myself.
To chart and compass this unfathomed sea,
Myself must plumb the boundless universe.
My Soul contains all thought, all mystery,
All wisdom of the Great Infinite Mind:
This to discover, I must voyage far,
At last to find it in my pulsing heart.

LOSS

But yesterday
The wealth of all the world
Did not exceed in value the great gift
That heaven to me did send:
Today
The humblest beggar in the land
Is infinitely richer than am I,
For I have lost—a friend.

ENTREATY

O, thou, who art more fair than words can tell
Or a fond lover's nimble fancy paint,
May I not come to thee, where thou dost dwell
With hope that thou wilt heed my mournful plaint?
O, Love, thou canst not choose but tender be,
Knowing my every heart-beat is for thee!

TOGETHER

O, come, Love, let us take a walk,
Down the Way-of-Life together;
Storms may come, but what care we,
If be fair or foul the weather.

When the sky overhead is blue,
Balmy, scented winds will after
Us, adown the valley blow
Haunting echoes of our laughter.

When Life's storms upon us beat
Crushing us with fury, after
All is done, there'll ringing come
Mocking echoes of our laughter.

So we'll walk the Way-of-Life,
You and I, Love, both together,
Storm or sunshine, happy we
If be foul or fair the weather.

SUNDAY ON GRASMERE LAKE

It was that sweet time we call the twilight hour,
On peaceful Grasmere Lake we idly rowed:
Before us, matchless beauty lay revealed
In sky and hill and gently sloping wood.

The myriad thoughts that to our lips came thronging
We could not speak, but all entrancéd sat
While at our boat in tender rhythmic cadence
The laughing, dancing wavelets softly tapped.

No scene in all creation could be sweeter!
The tiny cloud that o'er the hill-top hung,
The quiet vale, the brown dove-cote * half hidden
Would fire to song even the most halting tongue.

Small wonder that the poet was inspired
To sing of this fair spot he loved so well!
Not Bobbie Burns nor yet the Bard of Avon
Could of his haunts a lovelier story tell.

Then suddenly in voice deep and subduéd
One began the "Ode" of Wordsworth's to repeat,
"On Immortality," thus ending fitly
A holy day with holy joy complete.

---

* *Wordsworth's home is called Dove Cottage.*

LIFE AND DEATH

Life

I saw the candle brightly burning in the room!
The fringéd curtains gracefully draped back,
The windows, crystal clear!
Upon the generous hearth
Quick Wit and bubbling Laughter
  Flashed and danced,
  Sparkled and pranced,
And music to the glowing scene lent cheer.
It was a gracious sight,
So full of life, of love, of light!

Death

Then suddenly I saw a cloud of gloom
Take form within the room:
A blue-grey mist obscured the window-panes
And silent fell the *rout!*
Then from the shadows came the Dreaded Shape,—
The candle flickered out!

[54]

GOD

I know a lot of folk who think
That God
Is just a great, big tub
Of Grub.
Descanting on His bounty
They will measure
His prodigal treasure
By so many
"Head o' hogs," "bushel o' grain" or "barr'l o' potatoes!"

But to me
God is the lily's dream,
The low, sweet note
In the thrush's throat—
The sun-beam's glory by a dew-drop caught!
He is the mighty tide
Gripping old ocean's side—
The mountain's thought!

[55]

SPRING

Spring, thou wilful, changeful maid,
Venturesome, yet half afraid
King Winter to defy,
Come, with all thy airs and graces,
Perfumes sweet and flower-laces;
When he thy rare beauty faces,
He, of love, will die.

[56]

POETRY

What is poetry?
A thought of beauty—truth,
An emotion rife with ruth—
With love!
All rhythmically expressed,
Carefully groomed—exquisitely dressed.

ECSTASY

Your eyes star-worlds of beauty are,
My long road blazing from afar,
Sweet Emily!

The essence of the rose's musk
Bathes your wine-lips as through the dusk
They summon me!

The downy pillows of your breast,
Sweet Eden where my soul would rest
Eternally!

COMPENSATION

In my infinity of loss
I seek to find the gain,—
The tender glance, the word of love,
The kiss divine—in vain!
No priceless gem of memory,
But ah! the pain, the pain!

EGYPTIAN SPHINX

Inscrutable and awe-inspiring Sphinx,
Inimitable and immortal, whose
Majestic head of massed and matted kinks
Constrains alike the savant and the muse
To marvel at thy muted mystery!
What age-long memories thy face betrays!
What moving visions thou hast seen—*dost see!*
Thou art the symbol that, to present days,
The ancient years indubitably links!
Wherever men their righteous voices raise
Such deeds of grandeur to extol and praise,
The Sons of Africa, who builded thee,
Through us shall swell the song of jubilee:
And matchless thou shalt stand, imperial Sphinx.

[60]

BEAUTIFUL HANDS

To a Skilful Surgeon

Not perfectly moulded, not smooth and cold
Suggesting the touch of senseless gold,
But warm and pulsing hands, tenderly
Thrilling the wealth of a heart to me.

Hands that are willing and busy and warm;
Hands that are eager to shelter from harm;
Hands that are capable—potent indeed,
Quickly outstretched to another's need.

Ready and restful hands, loving and strong,
But soothing and soft as a lullaby song;
Hands with the magic given suffering to ease;
Oh, who would not worship such dear hands as these!

LINCOLN

*Upon the dedication of the Lincoln Memorial at
Washington, May 30, 1922*

Son of the people, softly, sweetly rest!
Thy universal heart felt all the woes
Of mankind! They only were thy foes
Who hated right—who loved the evil best:
How hard man's cruelty upon thee pressed,
Thy deeply-lined and tragic visage shows!
Thy great soul-agony, only God knows,
When this great Union's fate was put to test!
But trusting in Jehovah's power to guide,
Nor caring if the whole world should deride,
With granite will, thou stoodst the Right beside.
Thus from the lowly cabin thou didst climb
To hallow this memorial sublime,
And men shall love thee to the end of time.

OLD OCEAN AND THE SHORE

Lovers in Three Moods

I

Smiling, big and full of joy,
I saw Old Ocean rush upon the Shore:
With wide-spread arms
He caught her to his heart.
I heard him chuckle softly to himself;
I saw his fingers stroke her sea-weed hair;
He kissed and kissed and kissed again
Her lush, responsive lips!
  And she who had been pale and cold
  Grew warm and dimpled at his touch.

II

I saw Old Ocean sullen, moody, mad;
The Shore stretched out her shell-like hands in vain;
No bubbling laughter greeted her sad ear;
He offered no caress.
He glowered at her, grumbling through his teeth!
Oh, he was dark and sinister!
He would not look upon her, waiting, wan!
  God! I could better bear his blows
  Than this indifference!

[63]

III

I heard Old Ocean warring in his wrath!
He shook and slashed and swore with fury!
With heavy fists he beat upon the Shore;
He tore her hair;
He screamed and raged;
He bruised her tender, shining flesh;
He gripped her with the strength of many giants,—
Shrieking—lashing—kicking—
Until at length, his jealous fury spent,
He sank exhausted in her waiting arms!
  " *'Tis well,*" *the Shore said softly,*
  "*For he loveth much.*"

THE NEW YEAR

The New Year comes—fling wide, fling wide the door
Of Opportunity! the spirit free
To scale the utmost heights of hopes to be,
To rest on peaks ne'er reached by man before!
The boundless infinite let us explore,
To search out undiscovered mystery,
Undreamed of in our poor philosophy!
The bounty of the gods upon us pour!
Nay, in the New Year we shall be as gods:
No longer apish puppets or dull clods
Of clay; but poised, empowered to command,
Upon the Etna of New Worlds we'll stand—
This scant earth-raiment to the winds will cast—
Full richly robed as supermen at last!

Sincerely Yours,

Carrie Law Morgan Figgs

Poetic Pearls

BY

CARRIE LAW MORGAN FIGGS

1920
EDWARD WATERS COLLEGE PRESS
Jacksonville, Florida

CONT

INTRODUCTION

It has been the great desire of my heart to scatter sunshine and contribute something to the world.

Mine has not been a life of ease and pleasure, but toil and service.

I have given several years of service in the class room as a teacher and several years as Grand Most Ancient Matron of Heroines of Jericho, traveling and working among my people.

Hence it has been mine to observe much.

Therefore I am sending this little book out into th eworld.

I can not tell into whose hands this book may fall, but it is my sincere hope that every on ewho reads it will find· something interesting and inspiring.

C. L. M. F.

THIS BOOK IS LOVINGLY DEDICATED
TO MY MOTHER

POETIC PEARLS

TO MY MOTHER

Mother, the queenliest woman on earth,
Mother, the woman who gave me birth,
Mother, you made of me all that I am,
You fashioned my life by your own plan.

I notice, dear mother, your hair turning
    gray,
But your voice is the same as it was yes-
    terday;
Your eyes are as kind and your smiles
    are as sweet
As they were when I knelt years ago at
    your feet.

When storms rage around me and trou-
    bles roll high,
As of old, to your sheltering arms I fly;
You give me advice that I can't get from
    another,
Except Jesus, who is there on earth like
    a mother?

5

IT'S HARD TO KEEP A GOOD
MAN DOWN

The storm may rage, the wind may blow
  And beat him to the ground,
But one of the hardest things on earth
    to do
  Is to keep a good man down.

He may be white, he may be black,
  He may be red or brown;
He'll dodge your blow and grow and go,
  Because you can't keep a good man
    down.

Sometimes he can hardly lift his head,
  Oppression is his crown,
But when his heart is right God gives
    him light,
  And the world can't keep him down.

Friends may prove false, enemis succeed
  In building a mighty mound
Of treachery and slander,
  But none of these can hold a good man
    down.

This is a truth that friend and foe
  Alike have sought and found,
Regardless of what comes or go,
  You can't keep a good man down.

6

AFTER THE HONEYMOON

Said Johnnie Jenkins to his wife:
    Good evening, is it late?
You know it is, she hotly cried,
    Why now, it's half-past eight.

Says he, I am awful hungry, Jane,
    Make haste and fix my supper;
"Your supper? Why there's none to fix,
    Nothing here but bread and butter."

But where's those groceries, Jane, says
      he,
    I bought the other day?
"Pshaw! You talk like a crazy man,
    Can fifty cents worth last always?"

I don't like this way you are acting, Jane,
    You are entirely too extravagant,
As late as 'tis, now I must go
    And hunt a restaurant.

I am not used to cheap living, John,
    At home we had a-plenty,
You know that I had all heart could wish
    Till I was more than twenty.

He scratched his head and gave a sigh,
    While at her he madly stared,
You waste my labor as if though
    I was a millionaire.

7

Remember I am a poor man's son,
   What I get comes from my muscle,
And if things here don't make a change
   By Jove, you'll have to hustle.

I thought that when I married you
   'Twould better my condition,
But fifty cents a wek is worse
   Than a preacher on a mission.

So I can leave you and this hut
   And go back to my mother;
Says he: Well, here's your railroad fare,
   For I am tired of so much bother.

WHY SLIGHT THE WORKING GIRL?

I wish some one would tell me
   Why the working girl is slighted?
She may be as good as Virgin Mary,
   But to grand affairs she's not invited.

She works for an honest living,
   She appears both clean and neat,
But when the (so-called) best men meet her
   They snub her on the street.

They'll see her coming up the street,
   They'll stare her in the face,
Perhaps they'll speak,
   But to lift their hats they consider it a
      disgrace.

8

Every girl hasn't had the same chance,
  Some come from humble homes,
But they are just as pure and womanly
  As queens upon their thrones.

Does it make her any smaller
  Because she must work and face the
    world?
If her character is good, don't slight her
  Because she's a working girl.

Ofttimes she is a jewel,
  Sometimes a valued pearl,
Just give her a chance to prove it,
  And don't slight her, because she is a
    working girl.

THE BULL FROG'S SONG

On a stormy September morning,
  When first I heard the song,
It echoed through the village streets,
  As if from a mighty throng.

I caught it from the stable yard,
  It sounded through my room,
I hastened up, threw on my gown,
  As if wrapped in a magic swoon.

A big frog seemed to sing the bass,
  Another sang the tenor,
While dozens rang the alto's part,
  Hundreds led the soprano.

9

[113]

I stood there like some one amazed,
　　Till my brain began to tire,
From listening to this wonderous song
　　Sung by the woodland choir.

(This poem was written when the writer was
14 years of age.)

THE MEANEST MAN ON EARTH

You may talk about highwaymen
　　And of men of lowly birth,
But the man who robs a woman
　　Is the meanest man on earth.
He may steal gold and silver,
　　He may steal jewels rare,
He may steal crowns and kingdoms,
　　But nothing can compare
To a man who robs a woman
　　Of all that she holds dear.

She might be maid or matron,
　　She might be young or old,
She might be as poor as Lazarus,
　　Or she might have tons of gold,
She might be of the royalty,
　　Or she might be of humble birth,
But the man who steals her honor
　　Is the meanest man on earth.

There is a man who looks for goodness,
　　And then casts it to the wind,
There is a man who smiles like an angel

10

And his heart is as black as sin,
He seeks and finds the best home,
   Where all is joy and mirth,
He steals the sacred treasure,
   He is the meanest man on earth.

This mean man ought to be dealt with
   By legal and social laws,
He is more poisonous than the cobra,
   Like the tiger he has claws,
Drive him from society,
   In jail give him a berth,
Because the man who robs a woman
   Is the meanest man on earth.

CANE JUICE AND 'POSSUM
(Dialect)

Who is dat out dar knocking?
   Why, I am fixing to go to bed,
No, I ain't undressed,
   But I got my close off, combing my head.

Say you got sump'n to tell me?
   Well' won't dat sump'n keep?
No, I ain't so tired,
   'But I want to go to sleep.

Didn't quite understan' you,
   You got cane juice and 'possum, too?
Whar is you gwine, Sammy?
   You know I was teasin' to see what you
      would do.

11

You quit cuttin' up out dar, Sam,
  And come on in dis house;
You is jest a great big ole sweet baby
  Out dar trying to pout.

My, whar did you git dis 'possum?
  He's jest as fat as butter,
And dis good old cold sweet cane juice,
  Right fresh from de gutter?

Sam, I always did like you,
  'Cause I knowed dat you liked me,
And you've proved your love for me tonight
  By climbin' dat simmon tree.

And fetchin' me dis 'possum
  Over here in all dis cole,
You bet your life I'll be your wife,
  'Cause you is worth your weight in gole.

LAMENTATIONS OF A DECEIVED WOMAN

You have robbed me of virtue,
  You've robbed me of fame,
You have stolen my innocence
  And put me to shame;
Your smiles and your lies
  Just took hold of my heart
And forced me from honor
  And goodness to part.

Oh, why did I meet you?

12

Oh, why was I born?
Why didn't I die
   On that bright July morn?
When you swore your protection
   And promised your love,
I believed you as true
   As an angel above.

You plead with your lips,
   Then you plead with your eyes,
On your knees you beseeched me
   In a lover's pure guise;
With your arms you embraced meta
   You held me so tight,
'Til I forgot all the world
   In that moment of delight.

I loved you, but now I hate you,
   Look there at my child;
You deny it your name
   And the thought drives me wild;
I am forsakened by friends,
   I have been driven from home,
With my child I am an outcast,
   In this cold world alone.

O. God, you forgive,
   Please help me to forgive
This man who has robbed me
   Of all that life gives,
Of beauty and honor.
   Of joy and of mirth,
And has made me the most
   Miserable woman on earth.

13

TRIBUTE TO THE BUSINESS MEN OF JACKSONVILLE

If you ever visit Florida,
  Pray don't miss Jacksonville;
It is the place of all places,
  Where the Negro has climbed the hill.

There is a bunch of business men there
  Who really make things hum,
A. L. Lewis, J. H. Blodgett,
  And Charles H. Anderson.

W. J. Geter, B. C. Vanderhorst,
  And W. W. Parker, too,
Joe James and son and J. S. McLane,
  And Belton on Florida Avenue.

There's Abbott with his book store,
  Walker with his business college,
Don't forget the People's Drug Store,
  And Pratt filed with embalming knowl-
    edge.

They have some business women, too,
  Mrs. Madison Williams on the hill,
On Broad street Mrs. Kirkpatrick,
  Mrs. Sumpter and Mrs. McGill.

Then come to the professions,
  Such as doctors, lawyers and teachers,
They have them by the dozens,
  And scores of excellent preachers.

14

THE NEGRO HAS PLAYED HIS PART

When the days were cold and dreary,
  And America's future was looking dark,
Her black son marched forth with his gun,
  And boldly played his part.

He crossed the mighty ocean,
  He feared neither gas nor poisoned dart,
He wrote his name on the scroll of fame,
  And like other men played his part.

In every war that this country's been
  Blood dripped from the Negro's loyal
    heart.
At Bunker Hill, Ocean Pond, San Juan and
    Carrizal
  He certainly played his part.

Not only is he a fighter,
  He has a place in poetry, music and art,
Dunbar, Johnson and Tanner have proven
  That the Negro has played his part.

Then he yearned for education
  Of hand and head and heart,
Mary Bethune and Booker Washington tell
    us
  That in literature he plays his part.

Today finds him progressive,
  No more content with that ox cart,

15

He motors his car to his store or bank
And in commerce plays his part.

America, dear America,
Mother of all Americans thou art,
You need not grieve, your black boy won't
leave,
He's going to stay and continue to do his
part.

SONG DEDICATED TO THE HEROINES OF JERICHO

(Tune: America)

Heroines strong are we,
Sisters of Masons free,
Men of God's love;
Fighting for truth and right,
Walking in love's clear light,
Trusting for strength and might,
Our God above.

Being true, we can not fall,
He will uphold us all
With his strong arm;
Then let us march and pray,
Walk with Him day by day,
He'll safely lead the way,
Keep us from harm.

Heroines strong and bold,
Like heroines of old,

16

Rahab and Ruth,
We are a valiant band
Marchin gto glory land
Led by the guiding hand
   Of Christ the truth.

EASTER BELLS

Hark! What sound is this I hear?
   Such music it foretells,
The sound is soft, but sweet and clear,
   It must be Easter bells.

They ring and tell of Christ the Lord,
   Who conquered death and hell,
Then rose up to his blest above,
   Wonderful Easter bells.

Sweet bells, your music fills my soul
   And wraps me in a spell,
Your wondrous peals like ocean's roll,
   Oh! magical Easter bells.

Ring on, sweet bells,
   Ring loud and clear,
Help men to understand
   That Jesus Christ our Saviour dear
Broke death's cold iron band.

Tell them "He rose just as He said,"
   Spread it o'er vale and dell,
The joyful tidings onward spread,
   Ye heaven sent Easter bells.

17

Let every heart rejoice today,
  And crush in sin's hard shell,
And raise to heaven a joyous lay,
  As do these chiming Easter bells.

Ring on, sweet bells, ring more and more
  And hold me in your spell,
Until I reach that shining shore
  Where rings everlasting Easter bells.

A JEWEL PURE AND BRIGHT

Live so that the world will need you,
  Daily tread the path of light,
Keep a bag of sunshine with you,
  Be a jewel pure and bright.

Sow your seeds of sunshine hourly,
  They'll lodge in the proper spot;
And while thus you plant your sunshine
  You make easier some one's lot.

If a man, don't be a makeshift,
  Be a man, stand in the light,
Do the things that conscience tells you,
  Show the world that you can do right.

Never shirk or jump from duty,
  Walk right in and bear your part,
Help a brother lift his burden,
  And ofttimes you heal a bleeding heart.

18

If a woman, be a woman,
    Walk the path of truth and right,
Crown your life with priceless virtue,
    And be a jewel pure and bright.

Don't stop to look for temptations,
    They'll be thick on every hand;
Watch your step and press on forward,
    For truth and goodness take a stand.

And while thus you stand on duty,
    Watch the faces in the line;
When you see a sister faltering,
    Catch her, clasp her hand in thine.

Always keep your bag of sunshine,
    Sow the seeds both day and night,
And you'll help to make the world
    A garden of jewels pure and bright.

SAVE YOUR PENNIES

Listen, boys, I want to tell you,
    While to you I have the chance to speak,
While you are in the bloom of childhood,
    While the rose blooms in your cheek,
Be not idle, be not wasteful,
    But be diligent instead,
Save your pennies, they'll make dollars,
    Listen, boys, to what I've said.

Thrift and energy linked with labor
    Are sure to bring a just reward,

19

Round by round "you mount a ladder,'
  Step by step you cross a road,
Then let sun rise find you stirring,
  Let morning breezes fan your head,
And save your pennies, they'll make dollars,
  Hear me, for that's what I said.

If you stand alone, stand in your manhood,
  Stand for justice and for right,
Goodness clads a man with honor,
  Money clothes a man with might;
Then if you see a brother sinking,
  Save him, help him lift his head,
Show that you've a heart within you,
  Filled with love, that's what I said.

SATURDAY NIGHT

(Dialect)

I jes can't stan' it no longer,
  I want to ask is you losin' yo' mine?
Does you t'ink dat I is crazy?
  Or does you t'ink dat I is bline?
I kin count money jest as good as you kin,
  You only gim me eight dollars,
And try to make me b'l'eve it's ten.

Whut you done wid dem other two dollars,
    man?
  You can't fool me, I done heerd 'bout your
    plan,

20

You git it or I'll disgrace you sho,
  And you won't set on dat deacon's bench
    no mo.

You loss it? You nedn't start dat bluff,
I done heerd dat ole song long enough,
Every Saddy night you comes up short
Wid a blame long face and a game o' talk.

De man didn't pay you, or he is out o' town,
Or wor kgot scarce and dey cut wages down,
I knows all about it, an' you know whut fol-
    lers,
So you jest better git me dem other two dol-
    lars.

How's you gwine ter git it? I ought to ask
    you,
You knows whar it is, an' I does, too,
But if dat money dont' come in sight,
Man, you won't sleep in dis house tonight.

Whut you say? Now you know I ain't skeered
    o 'you,
If I wuz I'd be dead and buried ,too,
But dey aint no use o' all dis talk,
Git me dat money or take your clothes and
    walk.

'Cause I can work for myself and chillun,
    too,
To take your foolishness, I don't have it to
    do,
You found it, eh? Well, I's mighty glad,
'Cause I jest begin to feel myself gittin' mad.

21

ELBOWING

Please let me pass, I am in a hurry,
  My gracious, such a great crowd,
It is now half-past seven,
  I hear the town clock striking aloud.

Let you pass? Why, who's holding you?
  Just elbow your way through the crowd,
Everybody here is in a hurry,
  And nobody murmurs aloud.

If you stand back and wait for a clearing,
  While everybody else elbows his way,
You'll never get to your office,
  You'll stand on this corner all day.

But I don't like to jostle the ladies,
  And I don't like to squeeze between men,
But I must get away from this corner,
  Hark! I hear the clock striking again.

Everybody is in a great hurry,
  No one notices while you stand there,
Each one elbows his way to a clearing,
  Each one hurries to get him a share.

This world is a great busy thoroughfare,
  To succeed you must elbow your way,
If you wait for success to come to you,
  You'll wait there and die in dismay.

22

MY BROTHER'S KEEPER

Yes, I am my brother's keeper,
  I a mto help him bear his load,
I am to help him bridge the chasm,
  I am to help him build his road.

I am to cheer him when he is weary,
  I am to help him on his way,
I am to change his tears to gladness,
  I am to help him turn his night to day.

When his sky is thick and cloudy,
  Fringed with darkness, doubt and fear,
When the world seems black around him,
  'Tis my duty to be near.

I must lend a ray of sunshine,
  I must give a word of cheer,
I must make his pathway brighter,
  I must make his sky more clear.

HANNAH

Say, did you ever see Hannah?
  She is the prettiest girl in town.
She is not white, red or yellow,
  But she is a tantalizing brown.
Her eyes are like a charcoal,
  Her teeth like finest pearls,
Her smiles are like the dew-drops,
  Her hair, soft, lustrous curls.

23

When she goes to church on Sunday
  She's the center of attraction,
All eyes are fixed upon her,
  From the parson to the sexton.
She is the leader of the choir.
  You just ought to hear her sing,
And I believe that you'd agree with me
  That she is an angel without wings.

When the preacher calls for joiners,
  Hannah stands up and sings
"For you I am praying,"
  'Til she makes the welkin ring,
And even the hardest sinner
  Can not withstand that voice,
He rushes to the mercy seat
  And makes the church his choice.

You ought to go to Hannah's house,
  Everything shines like a pin,
Front room, bed room and kitchen,
  Alike they all are clean,
She meets you at the front door,
  With a smile and gentle manner;
And it puts your heart to thumping
  Just to get to speak to Hannah.

IN LOVING REMEMBRANCE OF MY FATHER, WHO DEPARTED THIS LIFE APRIL 15th, 1911

Dear father, thou hast left us here,
  In this world of sorrow, pain and crime,

24

For thee w eshed the orphan's tear,
  And God alone our wounds can bind.

Our love for thee can never die,
  Thy memory we will e'er adore,
O, sainted one, watch from on high,
  Till time shall cease and be no more.

Watch for the five thou hast left behind,
  'Til death shall bring us all to thee,
Some day, I do not know the time,
  We, too, must cross the mystic sea.

Somewhere beyond "the vale of tears,"
  I do not know just where 'twill be,
But where God lives through endless years.
  With the I'll spend eternity.

Sleep on, O, sainted one, sleep on,
  We know thou art sleeping with the blest,.
For thy labors thou hast won a crown,
  So sleep, dear father, take thy rest.

CHRIST'S PERSON

(Written for and accepted by the A. M. E.
Church Review ,October Number, 1917)

"The fairest among ten thousand altogether lovely" is perhaps the sanest description of the personality of Christ that language can express.

25

Being altogether lovely is snyonymous to being completely lovely, perfect in this, attainment without possible improvement.

While being superlatively fair he again transcends the sphere of human conception and soars into the realms of that infinite wisdom reserved only for the Gods, for truly Christ is the Son of God.

Science tells us that in the attempted classification of objects or qualities the mind is incapable of comprehension unless there is a comparing object of known characteristics. Since there are no other beings save the Divine Trinity that possess such personal characteristics, all efforts of a description of Christ's personal qualities can but fail.

The fall of man in the Garden of Eden through disobedience necessitated the descension of Christ to earth to redeem man from his lost state. Preparatory to his coming men were divinely inspired to prophesy the future birth of a promised Messiah. Chief among these was Isaiah, who nine hundred years prior thereto, in an effort to set before the world a true conception of his majesty, thus proclaims: "For unto us a child is born, unto us a son is given, and the government shall be upon his shoulder. His name shall be called Wonderful, Counsellor, the Mighty God, the Everlasting Father, the Prince of Peace.

Wonderful beyond human comprehension

26

for the power to know Christ must come from above, for thus said Christ unto Peter when Peter declared thou art the Christ, the Son of the living God. "Flesh and blood did not reveal this unto you." Counsellor, a friendly advisor, telling to us what to do, why we should and how to do his command. Even here is he wonderful, for so great and complete is his friendship that he counted his own life not dearer to him than his friends.

The mighty God, having power over all creation, in heaven, on earth and over hell. The everlasting Father, unlimited in time, a father whose duration outstrips time and eternity. Yet through his matchless love, in perfect obedience, he descnds from his great white throne and became subject t othe laws of earth ,even to the law of condemnation imposed upon man pursuant to his disobedience, and died the ignominous death of the cross that man might be saved.

The Immaculate Christ, in his sublime divinity, is without physical personality, for God is a spirit, possessing a spiritual body, complete in all that is essential in true divinity.

Thus may I conclude with this assertion, so pure, so perfect, so holy and divine is Christ that language is incapable of conveying to us a true picture of His personality, nor can human wisdom conceive its won-

27

·drous beauty and perfection.

For beauty there is none like him,
    For strength there is none so strong,
His presence drives sin out of us,
    And turns our grief to song.

For love, who can with him compare
    With the great love he has shown?
He laid aside his royal crown
    And descended from his throne.

He came to earth, He bled and died
    On rugged Calvarys tree,
He took the contract, paid the price
    With His blood and made us free.

WELCOME ADDRESS DELIVERED TO THE SEVENTH QUADRENNIAL SESSION OF WOMAN'S MITE MISSIONARY SOCIETY, OCT. 15th, 1919.

Mistress of Ceremonies, Honored Bishop,
    Distinguished Visitors, Ladies and Gentlemen:
    I am delighted to have this privilege to welcome you here tonight in behalf of the North Jacksonville District.
    We have not come to tell you of obstacles and sorrows that confront us and thereby make you sad, but we have come with hearts filled with love to bring you greetings and to

28

tell you how welcome you are in our midst and if possible make you glad that you came to the Land of Sunshine and Roses. It is our intention, ladies and gentlemen, to see to it that while you sojourn here among us that your stay be one of pleasure.

It cheers the heart of a stranger to recive a cordial welcome.

People have been exchanging visits with each other and extending and acepting words of welcome ever since way back in the early ages of the world.

When Magda, the Queen of Sheba, visited Solomon, he greeted her with words of welcome, such as she had never heard before.

When Ruth left the land of Moab, the land of her nativity and went with her mother-in-law, Naomi, to live in Judah she was welcomed heartily by the people of Judah and doubly welcomed by Boaz in whose field she gleaned, and who later became her husband.

When Esther, the Jewish maiden, who was made Queen of Persia, and who risked her life to enter uninvited the court of Ahaseurus to visit him and to plead for her people, was made to reioice, because of the welcome accorded her by the king when he extended to her the golden scetper and bade her to make her wishes known and that they should be granted evn unto the half of his kingdom.

We have no kingdom to offer or lay at your disposal, but we have many other things

29

of which we are justly proud and in behalf of the North Jacksonville District I am happy to say to you that to all of these you are welcome.

We are glad to have you here to see the wonderful achievements that we have made, morally, intellectually, financiallyand spiritually.

Under the leadership of our distinguished, intelligent, dignified Christian bishop, the Right Revernd John Hurst, the general of the Eleventh Episcopal District, who has been so nobly supported by these gallant, untiring, unselfish, ever-ready presiding elders, pastors and laymen, we have brought things to pass and our fondest dreams have been realized, and if you doubt my statements, all that you need to do is to look about you, see this, Mt. Zion Church, see Edward Waters College, see the report for missions and other things, and you will agree with me that you are being welcomed by a great people of a great church in a great district, the greatest district in all Florida, presided over by one of the most scholarly presiding elders in the entire connection in the person of Dr. Daniel M. Baxter.

So, again, I want to say to you that:

You are welcome, yes, indeed, you are,
Welcome as the morning star
Was to the wise men of the East
When they sought for the Prince of Peace.

30

You are as welcome as the breeze of May,
You are as welcome as a summer day,
You are as welcome as the birds that sing,
You are as welcome as the flowers of spring.

We welcome you because you are
Moral and spiritual guiding stars,
Lifting others as you climb,
To heights above sin, shame and crime.

Because you are helping to mold and make
Better men and women for humanity's sake,
Because like giants you've taken a stand
To fight down wrong where'er you can.

Because you fear neither heat nor cold,
Because you are Christians strong and bold,
Because you've heard the heathen's cry,
Because you've answered, "Here am I."

Because you know no east or west,
Because you are striving to do your best,
Because you are treading the path our Savior
      trod,
Because we are all children of the living God.

You are welcome to our glad sunshine,
You are welcome to our corn and wine,
You are welcome to our milk and honey,
And you are welcome even to our money.

31

You are welcome to our broad, clean streets,
You are welcome to our bread and meats,
And if cooked food fails your taste to suit,
You are welcome to our groves of fruit.

Oranges, mangoes, lemons, grapes and limes,
Sugar apples, paupaus and apples called
    pines,
Sea grapes, cocoanuts and bananas not a
    few,
Alvacado pears, plums and guavas, too.

To food and shelter, to carriage and car,
To all that we have you are welcome, yes, you
    are,
Now, if there is aught in my welcome left un-
    said,
Charge it not to the heart, please, but charge
    it to the head.

Because if each of us had a thousand tongues
We would gladly welcome you with every
    one,
So with hearts as pure as heaven's own dew,
In Jehovah's name we welcome you.

32

Nuggets of Gold

by

Carrie Law Morgan Figgs
(Author of "POETIC PEARLS")

Price 50 cents

Chicago, Illinois

CONTENTS

PREFACE

DEAR READER,

The enormous sales of "Poetic Pearls" has inspired me to send to you "Nuggets of Gold", "Poetic Pearls" met with such popular favor until I've received some very beautiful letters complimenting them.

We give a few extracts below:

Rev. John A. Gregg A. M., D. D. President of Wilberforce University says:

'Poetic Pearls' is a very fine contribution, I'am very much pleased with it.

Rev. J. C. Caldwell, ex-secretary Allen Christian Endeavor League, says:

The book is a contribution to the literature of our race.

Hon. Charles H. Anderson, Capitalist and banker, says:

This book is entitled to a place in a class with the best poems of the world.

Rev. John W. Jones, Associate Editor of The Fla. Times Union, says:

"Poetic Pearls" scatters sunshine and point out ten shining points on the checkered pathway of life.

Madame Victoria Clay Haley, says:

I feel sure that much inspiration will be gained by the reading of these pages. The first two selections alone are worth the price of the book.

Rev. Arthur L. James, pastor First Baptist Church, Roanoke, Va., says:

7

It is not only production of literary merit, but it is soul deep in its rich contributions toward helping the world to become sweeter, kinder, safer and happier.

Major R. R. Jackson, Chicago Alderman and Major General of Knights of Pythias, says:

The book is a jewel. You are the uncrowned queen of literary art.

Dr. S. G. Baker, Editor of "The Messenger", says:

This production places Madame Figgs in the school of poets, and should be read by all.

I hope that "Nuggets of Gold" will inspire you as does a golden nugget when dropped into your palm, and meet your kind approval as does "Poetic Pearls".

C. L. M. F.

8

MY NUGGETS OF GOLD

I own three golden nuggets.
  Two boys and a girl;
Who fondly call me mother;
  I'm the happiest woman in the world.

I loved them ere they knew me,
  I prayed that they might live;
As their little brown arms entwined me,
  I gave all that I could give.

A mother's love and sympathy;
  A mother's joy and tears;
A mother's heart—felt interest,
  And above all, a mother's prayers.

I heard their childish laughter,
  I joined them in their play;
I kissed their cuts and bruises;
  I wiped their tears away.

God has let me keep my nuggets,
  Til now they are lumps of gold;
I pray that He will refine them,
  And when life is over take them into his
                                    [fold.

9

A PRAYER

1

Father of the fatherless,
  Friend of the poor,
Husband for the widow,
  Open hopes' door.

2

Thou hast heard us pray
  In days gone by;
Hear us now Father;
  Heed Thou our cry.

3

Thou art Almighty,
  We know Thou art God,
All men are thy children,
  Their Mother the sod.

4

Thou didst lead Israel
  From Egypt's dark land,
Lead us O Father;
  Grant us thy hand.

5

Make America safe for Democracy,
  Safe for black as well as other men;
Hear us O Father,
  We beg thee—Amen.

10

LIFE

1

A moment of pleasure,
  An hour of pain,
A day of sunshine,
  A week of rain,
A fortnight of peace,
  A month of strife,
These taken together
  Make up life.

2

One real friend
  To a dozen foes,
Two open gates,
  'Gainst twenty that's closed,
Prosperity's chair,
  Then adversity's knife;
These my friends
  Make up life.

3

At daybreak a blossom,
  At noontime a rose,
At twilight 'tis withered,
  At evening 'tis closed.
The din of confusion,
  The strain of the fife,
These with other things
  Make up life.

4

A smile, then a tear,
  Like a mystic pearl,
A pause, then a rush

11

[145]

Into the mad whirl,
A kiss, then a stab
From a traitor's knife;
I think that you'll agree with me,
That this life.

LOVE

Something that makes you feel
  Like a fool half the time.
Something that makes you act
  Like a mule when he's blind.
Something over which you have
  Absolutely no control,
Something that makes your blood hot,
  And then it makes it cold.

2

Something that dulls your senses,
  And then sometime make them keen
Something that makes you kind and sweet,
  But sometimes makes you mean.
Something that makes the eyes soft.
  And makes the heart beat fast.
Something that clings to memory
  In the ctiy of the past.

3

Something that's high and holy,
  Then sometimes it's mean and low,
But it will make you leap through fire,
  It will make you wade through snow,
It will make you cross the ocean,
  It will make you mount the air;
It will make you cross the desert;

12

It will make you curse and swear.

4

Something that makes you happy,
  Then sometimes it makes you sad.
Something that makes you beetter,
  Then semotimes it makes you bad.
It was this that made Adam
  Have to leave his Eden home,
And 'twas this that made Ahasuerus
  Bring Esther to his throne.

5

Something that's high as heaven,
  Something deeper than a well.
Something so mysterious
  That wise men fail to tell.
It makes of you a lion,
  Then it makes of you a dove
This mysterious thing I speak of
  Is, L O V E, love.

WHOA MULE
(Dialect)

1

Whoa mule; aint you got no sense?
  Keep jammin dis cart up to dis fence
Don't you know you'll break it down?
  You's de biggest fool mule in dis town.

2

Anybody dat looks at you
  Can see you is country thru and thru
A city mule has got some sense
  You never see him jammin de fence.

13

3

When his boss says to him "be still"
  He, stops right then and obeys his will
He gently turns his head around
  To see if his boss is on the ground.

4

He stands up jes where he is placed
  He looks a street car in de face
He winks at autos passing by
  From motorcycles he will not shy.

5

I know you've seen a car befo,
  Don't you hear me keep saying whoa!!
I'll take dis stick and bust yo hide,
  You act so daw-gonned country-fied.

6

Now when I get up from my seat,
  You stand bolt upright on yo feet;
And let these city mules find out,
  That you are not a country clout.

7

Mule, are you really trying to pout,
  Or are you trying to pitch me out?
The mo I talk to you bout sense;
  The mo you jams into this fence.

8

You think that you'll have some fun,
  But mule, my business you can't run;
I'll tell you when I want to go,
  Stand up I tell you; I mean whoa!!

14

ROLLING WATERS

1

Rolling waters, tell me true,
  Just how long you've 'ashed and rolled
Rolling waters deep and blue,
  Really are you very old?

2

Rolling waters, I know you.
  Yet, of you I am so afraid;
Tell me of the things you do
  Tell me of the graves you've made.

3

Then the waters answered me,
  "I was here ere God made man
The God of heaven named me "Sea"
  And called your place of abode, land.

4

Upon my bosom fishes play,
  Upon my bosom storms do ride
Within my bowels treasurers lay
  That I swallowed with fiendish pride.

5

I swallow ships, I swallow men;
  I give them a bed upon my floor
To sleep and never wake again
  'Til time shall cease and be no more.

6

Man is to rule all things on land,
  Man can tame the lion bold;
But I wish man to understand
  That o'er me, he has no control.

15

7

I leap, I dash, I rise and fall,
   I allow your ships to ride my foam;
At times I am a chasm then a wall;
   I obey God and God alone.

8

All men to me are just the same,
   I treat the rich as I do the poor,
I care not for their wealth or fame
   They are men to me and nothing more.

9

I leap, I dash, I rise and fall
   I allow your ships to ride my foam;
I heed nobody's cry or call,
   I obey God and God alone.

THE NEGRO'S UPWARD FLIGHT

1

As the eagle soars skyward
   Each day in her flight
The Negro soars upward
   From darkness to light.

2

He has flown from his cabin
   His banjo and pranks
To position and honor
   To title and rank.

3

His brother in white
   Is no longer his peer
He is the equal of any man
   Found anywhere.

16

4

He left slavery's shore
  And for knowledge he sought
Today he is a giant
  In the city of thought.

5

He is not begging for favors
  Along so called social lines
He wants equal rights
  For this only, he pines.

6

He's a citizen in peace
  He is a soldier in the war's din
But he asks for the treatment
  That is given to other men.

WE ARE MARCHING

1

We are marching, truly marching
  Can't you hear the sound of feet?
We are fearing no impediment
  We have never known defeat.

2

Like Job of old we have had patience,
  Like Joshua, dangerous roads we've trod
Like Solomon we have built out temples.
  Like Abraham we've had faith in God.

3

Up the streets of wealth and commerce,
  We are marching one by one
We are marching, making history,
  For ourselves and those to come.

17

4

We have planted schools and churches,
   We have answered duty's call.
We have marched from slavery's cabin
   To the legislative hall.

5

Brethren can't you catch the spirit?
   You who are out just get in line
Because we are marching, yes   we   are
      marching
   To the music of the time.

6

We are marching, steady marching
   Bridging chasms, crossing streams
Marching up the hill of progress
   Realizing our fondest dreams.

7

We are marching, truly marching
   Can't you hear the sound of feet?
We are fearing no impediment
   We shall never know defeat.

SIGNS

If a black cat cross your way,
   You'll have bad luck all day.
If you meet a cross-eyed man,
   You might as well change your plan.
If your left eye jumps,
   You are going to have some awful bumps.
If you strike your right foot big toe,
   Into trouble you are bound to go.
If you put your hat on the bed,

18

Disappointments are ahead.
If there's an itching of the right hand,
    You'll get a letter from a man.
If the left hand itch its funny,
    But you'll surely get some money.
If you dream of the dead,
    Rain is not far ahead.

THE BLACK QUEEN

All hail! this honest dusky maid,
    Let all others prostrate fall;
Bring forth the international diadem,
    And crown her queen of all.

In all pure womanly qualities,
    She stands serene and tall,
Way up above the average,
    This makes her queen of all.

She's not a sluggard at any place,
    She answers duty's call
Come all ye people, small and great,
    And crown her queen of all.

She stands bolt upright by her men,
    She will not let them fall,
Now for her valor, tip your hat,
    And crown her queen of all.

19

DEAR OLD HOME OF MINE

1

Tis true I've moved far from you
  Into another cline
But there is no place just like you
  Dear old home of mine.

2

I've made many new friends
  They invite me out to dine
There are no friends like home friends,
  Dear old home friends of mine.

3

I love your smiling waters
  I love your sun kissed clime
I love your vales and meadows
  Dear old home of mine.

4

I love your grassy meadows
  I still hear the whispering pine
I fancy that I hear song-birds singing
  In that dear old home of mine.

5

At night I dream of old friends,
  With love their faces shine
The smiles and hand shakes thrill
  In that dear old home of mine.

20

A TEMPERANCE POEM

1

Temperance is a holy cause;
  It teaches naught but love,
The God who rules the universe
  Indorses it above.

2

The wine cup is dangerous,
  It makes you from good breeding part,
It drags you down to ruin,
  And takes possession of your heart.

3

I wouldn't be a drunkard's wife
  I hate the maddening cup,
It taints your morals, wrecks your life;
  And drinks your senses up.

4

Oh Temperance, Temperance wonderous
  name
  That reaches men in every clime
That lifts them from their walks of shame
  And makes them walk in paths sublime.

5

Great God protect the Temperance cause;
  Shelter it neath thy mighty wing;
Defend those who uphold its laws,
  So of sweet Temperance they might
    sing.

21

NANCY

1

Nancy is a nurse sir
  She's just as fine as silk
She is always bright and smiling,
  But she insists on giving you milk,
Says she, "It's the doctor's orders"
  That you shall have no meat:
She fills you with the liquid
  While the chicken she does eat.

2

She opens wide your mouth sir,
  And your temperature she takes,
Then she writes down something funny
  In a booklet that she makes
Just to show the doctor
  How well you are thriving
And to impress upon him greatly,
  To obey him she is striving.

3

You can tell when the doctor's coming
  Nancy sticks down her hair
Then she paints and powders her face sir
  Until she is beautiful and fair
She bathes your face and gently rubs
  The wrinkles from your cheek
She says: "now dearie lie quite still
  And to doctor do not speak."

4

She warns you "now be careful"
  Be quiet as a mouse
Look wise and smile quite cheerful

22

The doctor's in the house"
To keep you from telling doctor
That all the chicken she did eat
She tells him that you are delirious
And strange things do repeat.

5

Nancy really knows her business,
She is loving clean and neat
She will nurse you back to life sir,
But your goodies she will eat.
She will read you fairy stories,
She'll take you to the land of Fancy
While she eats your chicken, cream and
cake,
This mystifying Nancy.

I WILL TRUST IN JESUS
(Sacred)

1

Tho my path be dark as night,
I will trust in Jesus.
Tho I see no ray of light,
I will trust in Jesus.

2

Tho my sky be thunder riven,
I will trust in Jesus.
He looks down upon me from high heaven
I will trust in Jesus.

3

Tho my cheeks be bathed with tears,
I will trust in Jesus.
He can carry all of my cares,
I will trust in Jesus.

23

I will trust him all the way,
My friend, my Savior, Jesus.
Until I reach that "Perfect Day",
I will trust in Jesus.

WHO'S YOU TALKIN TO
(Dialect)
1

Boy! I'll split you wide open,
You gitten yo sef some brass;
Everytime I open my mouf to you,
You got to gim-me a game o sass.

2

I always thought you'd be nothin,
You low lifed ugly villun;
You is mo like your old daddy
Than any of my other chillun.

3

What you say? you glad you like him?
Shut up! don't talk back to me,
Didn't you hear me say shut up you rascal,
Why I'll beat you 'til you can't see.

4

Why I'LL break you down in the loins sir
If you gimme any mo' talk
Don't you think that I can't reach you
Cause I got rheumatiz and can't walk.

5

Now stop dat sniffin and cryin'
Take yo' sleeve and wipe dem nose
Stop dat humpin in yo' shoulders
Straighten out dem crooked toes.

24

6

Go on on' clean dat kitchen.
    Wash every dish pot an' pan
Don't you roll yo' eyes at me sir
    Remember you aint no man.

7

Lawd have mercy on dat boy
    You know Lawd I aint mad
But I have to scare him up like dat
    Cause he is so everylasting bad.

THE MURDERER

1

John Jones and Fred Pratt had a falling out;
    It was all about Nellie Brown;
Nell liked Jones better than she did Pratt,
    So of course she turned Pratt down.

2

Says Pratt: "Miss Brown, Jones is a thief,
    He served three years on the gang;
He is only a common rousta bout;
    Pardon me for such slang.

3

I know for when my father was County
    Judge, he sentenced Jones three times;
Once for stealing a box of hams,
Once for stealing a dime
    And the third time for stealing a little
    girl not past the age of nine".

4

Now this was a malicious lie;
    Nell unlike most girls could see

25

So she said " you are a coward Pratt
    To speak such words to me".
                    5
"Father says that John is a gentleman
    And I think he ought to know
For they were in business together
    In the Klondike Eleven long years or more
                    6
"And further more I want to tell you
    To save contention and strife
That with a heart filled with love
    I have promised to be no other than
        John Jone's wife.
                    7
These words sank deep into Pratt's mean
        soul,
    Thought he, "It shall never be
Before he shall marry the girl I love
    I'll send his soul to eternity".
                    8
Pratt knew the road that Jones used
    When he went to see Miss Brown,
He hid himself behind the trees,
    Just outside the town.
                    9
Jones came walking along slowly,
    Thinking "to-morrow Nell will be my
        bride"
When suddenly Pratt sprang
    From the shrubery by his side.
                    10
He felled Jones with a bludgeon;
                    26

Then stabbed him to the heart,
Then dragged his body from the road
To a safe place in the dark.

11

He crept back through the shrubery,
He fled into his home;
But the eyes of God were upon him;
He felt he was not alone.

12

Next day the constable sought him
And confronted him with his crime;
"You were seen" he told the murderer
"By eyes more keen than mine".

13

The day that they had the trial,
Nell's face was calm but firm;
Neath her searching gaze Pratt faltered;
Like a worm he did squirm.

14

The Judge gave out this sentence,
"You shall hang 'til you are dead"
They marched the prisoner outside,
To the gallows he was led.

15

He knelt in meditation;
"Forgive me God," he said.
He drove a dirk into his own heart;
At the sheriff's feet he fell dead.

27

THE PICNIC

1

We had a wonderful time at the picnic;
   Everybody in town was there.
We sang and played and frolicked
   'Til our music filled the air.

2

Joe Brown was there with his sister;
   And Ned was there with his gal
Yes Sam was there with Mirandy;
   Pete Jenkins he brought Sal.

3

Parson Jones he brought the widow
   A leanin on his arm,
You could see that he was frightened;
   But he tried to look quite calm.

4

The young folks started dancing;
   Parson lifted his glasses and said,
"Suppose we don't do that children
   Let's have the grand march instead".

5

"Good" came a chorus of voices,
   Let the parson lead the march;
The parson walked out boldly,
   But his face was as white as starch.

6

The marchers walked out gracefully,
   Each couple took its place;
Phil Tomkins gave the orders
   With perfect ease and grace.

28

The band was playing Dixie,
  The parson looked left then right,
His partner had gotten away from him,
  And was almost out of sight.
You know the widow can't see well;
  And she grabbed Joe Bown by the arm
Thinking that twas the parson
  Who was holding her by his charm.
Parson got Joe Brown's sister,
  And she's gay young thing;   .
When he found himself she had him
  Actually cutting the pigeon wing.
The young folks caught the spirit,
  But when the parson tried to stop;
His feet refused to help him,
  So on the floor he fell ker flop.
Now by him falling suddenly,
  It made us all fall down;
And my slipper heels were caught
  In the wig of Fannie Brown.
Well say, did she look funny?
  Everybody began to laugh;
Her head looked like an apple
  When it is split in half.
I couldn't get my slipper
  From the tangles of that hair;

29

Imagine me a limping
　　Around with my right foot bare.
14
We finally found our places
　　And got back into line;
But child I want to tell you
　　We had one jolly time.

THAT EASTERN STAR

(Sacred)

That star of joy and hope
　　That star of love divine
That star of light and peace and life
　　That shines for all mankind.
2
Our star reminds of Him
　　Who died on Calvary's tree
Whose blood can cleanse from every sin
　　And make the bondsman free.
3
That star shone through the past
　　It will shine for years to come
Its beams have led us through the blast
　　Its beams will lead us home.
4
Dear guiding star above
　　Of thee, to thee we sing
Lead us with the rays of love
　　While to thy points we cling.

30

SMILE, WORK AND SING

Smile and the world grows better,
    Smile and upon gloom put a fetter,
Smile and open friendships letter;
    Smile, Smile, it's a deal of fun.

Work and the task grows lighter
    Work, and your sun shines brighter
Work, and your grip grows tighter
    On success, and you're sure to win.

Sing and you help your brother,
    Sing, you lift the cloud for another
Sing and evil thoughts you smother
    From the recesses of your heart.

31

SELECT PLAYS

Santa Claus Land

Jepthah's Daughter

The Prince of Peace

Bachelors' Convention

By
CARRIE LAW MORGAN FIGGS
Author and Publisher

Notice:-Production of these Plays is FREE to Amateurs, but the sole *Professional Rights* are reserved by the *Author*. *Moving Picture Rights* reserved.

Young Print, 5207-9 State St, Tel. Oakland 4942

SANTA CLAUS LAND

Lights Out in Audience, But Soft Yellow Lights on Platform—Star Above Manger

Green and Yellow Lights on Stage—Brown Leaves and Sticks on Floor

CHARACTERS

Queen of Fairies and Fairies
King of Goblins and Goblins
Santa Claus
Mrs. Santa Claus
Children
Alice, the Children's Governess
Fluffy
Stuffy
Toughy

Act I.

Trees Covered with Ice and Snow

Goblins in the woods. (6)
Children in the woods.
Fairies in the woods. (12)

Children wandering here and there drop carelessly on ground.

Alice—I am so tired! We've wandered all day in this dreary wood looking for holly berries and Santa Claus Land. I wonder if there really is a Santa Claus and a Santa Claus Land?

Voice from behind the trees: "Yes, there is a Santa Claus and there is a Santa Claus Land."

Children start: "What is that? Who is that? Alice —did you hear that?"

Alice—Yes, I heard it. Who are you and where are you?

Voice—I am Queen of the Fairies. I am in the air. Look about you.

Children look in every direction. Queen appears.

[169]

Queen—Well, children dear, what are you doing here? Do you know that you are miles away from home? Do I understand that you are looking for Santa Claus Land?

Children—Yes, good lady, but who are you? Are you Queen of the Fairies?

Queen—Yes, I am Queen of the Fairies, and you are now in Fairy Land, but since 't is Christmas Eve, you are looking for **Santa Claus Land?**

Fluffy—Yes, but we'd like to stay here long enough to see the fairies.

Children—Yes! yes! Let us see the Fairies! Are they all pretty like you?

Queen—You shall see them. (Waves wand.) Fairies, Fairies, blithe and free; Fairies, Fairies, come to me. 1, your Queen, am calling thee; for these children here, to see—they have never seen and known Fairies from the flowers blown, but I am calling thee tonight. Come, come quickly into sight.
Fairies flit in, holding garlands of Holly, and gather around Queen.

Faires, Queen Mother—Here we are at thy command. We were busy heart and hand, weaving garlands fresh and gay to crown our brows on Christmas day.

Fluffy—Gee, what pretty Fairies! Are all Fairies pretty like these?

Stuffy—I wish I could eat one of them. I am so hungry. Are they good to eat?

Toughy—Boy, ain't you got no sense? Them's nothing but gals. They ain't no Fairies. Them's home made wings; watch me catch one of 'em and take them wings off.

Alice—Why, Toughy, I am ashamel of you. Keep still.

Toughy creeps up and examines Fairies wings: "I told you so."

Alice pushes Toughy aside and says: "Queen, we were looking for holly brances; can we get some of your garlands?"

Queen walks over to Alice and puts garland on Alice's head, and says: "Now, you are Queen of the children. You all may have these garlands; the Fairies will make some more for their use. (Fairies give children garlands)

Children all: "Thanks, thanks, but how can we get to Santa Claus Land?"

Queen—Dear children, Santa Claus Land is not far, but you will have to pass through the Land of the Goblins, and they are very fierce. But it is interesting to see them at work—they make Christmas toys.

Alice—O Fairy Queen, can't you go with us? We're afraid.

Queen—I must stay in my own land.

Toughy—Have no fear, Alice. I can lick any Goblin that ever lived. Follow me. We'll go there and see the toys and pass on through. Come on, Stuffy.

Curtain

Act II.

In the Land of Goblins

Goblins at work making Christmas toys, horns, drums, dolls, etc. One stands on guard at door with sword. King sits on throne. Children peep in timidily. Toughy enters, followed by children—he's full of Goblins he ate on the way here. And Fluffy lights on Goblins' heads and picks their eyes out.

King of the Goblins—And what do you do, young man?

Toughy—I lick a hundred Goblins at a time.

King—Have you seen the Fairies?

Alice—Yes, they gave us these garlands. They were very nice to us.

King—Your voice is so soft, and your eyes so gentle, until I would like to keep you here and make you queen of the Goblins. The others may go—but you must stay.

Alice—Toughy! Toughy, he says that I must stay. Toughy, please take me away. O Toughy! Toughy!

Children—O sir, please let her come with us.
Toughy—Alice will come with us.

King lifts his hand. Toughy knocks King down; other Goblins rush in. Toughy whips them all. Takes Alice by hand and starts to lead her and other children out.

King—You cannot gain admission to Santa Claus Land without my seal upon your forehead. Santa is my friend.

Toughy—We don't need your seal. Goodby, Goblins Hope you'll know how to act when another band of children pass through your land. Goodby, old King.

Curtain

Act II.
(Scene 2)

Toy Shop in Santa Claus Land

Santa Claus and Mrs. Santa Claus, both filling stockings
    and baskets—all kinds of toys on shelves or table
Children knock loudly on door.

Mrs. Santa—Who knocks there? We are very busy tonight.

Voices from without—We are a band of children looking for Santa Claus.

Mrs. Santa—Come in.

Children enter.

All clap hands and dance gaily about. "O this is Santa Claus' toy shop! Look at the pretty toys!"

Mrs. Santa—What and who are you?

(Someone moving small mirrors which will cause reflections on walls to resemble sunbeams. Little girls chasing and scattering and chasing sunbeams.)

First Little girl:
    We are little children
    From the land of dreams

And our occupation is
To scatter bright sunbeams.

Second Little Girl:

All is joy and pleasure
Where the firelight gleams,
But our happiest moments
Are when chasing bright sunbeams.

Third Little Girl:

We traverse hills and valley,
We cross the rippling streams;
We fear not wind or weather,
We always find sunbeams.

Fourth Little Girl:

We take them to poor children
Where all is dark it seems,
And with kind words softly sjoken,
We slip them bright sunbeams.

Fifth Child:

We are so gay and happy
Because in our hearts love beams,
And though we are little children
The world calls us sunbeams.

All:

So we are little children
From the land of dreams—
And our occupation is
To scatter bright sunbeams.

Santa Claus—Good evening, children. We are very glad to see you. Rest yourselves and then look around.

Mrs. Santa—Children, are you hungry? I have some cookies (gives each of the children a cooky and pats each on shoulder.)

Alice—This is wonderful. O, how I should like to stay here.

Toughy—Got any more cookies, madam? You are some good cook.

Stuffy—Yes, I'd like to have another one, too—please, ma'm.

Alice—Toughy, I am ashamed of you and Stuffy.

Toughy—You weren't ashamed of me when them Goblins was after you, and you're ashamed now? Well, stay ashamed, if you stay ashamed you won't get hungry.

Santa Claus—Come now, children, and see the toys and joys of Santa Claus Land.

Children look joyfully into every nook and corner.

Alice—How wonderful! O, why can't we stay here always?

Children—No, Alice, we must go back and tell the other children of the beauties of Santa Claus Land.

Fluffy—Mrs. Santa Claus can we have some toys to take with us to the children?

Mrs. Santa—Yes, dear, but what is your name?

Fluffy—My name is Fluffy and these are my brothers, Toughy and Stuffy. They are wonderful boys. And that big pretty girl is Alice. She is our governess. O, but we must soon go!

Children—O, such pretty toys.

Santa—Here are toys for each of you (gives each toys) and you had better hy away, because we must go and take gifts to the children in your land.

(Sleigh bells are heard in the distance.)

Children—O, listen to the bells. Santa Claus, is that your sleigh outside?

Santa—Yes, be on your way, little dears, and I will visit you in your homes while I am in your land.

Santa and Mrs. Santa exit, each carrying large bag of toys.

Curtain

Jepthah's Daughter

Costumes

Jepthah - 1st. act simple robe and sandals short stocky beard, cropped wig.

3rd act. -- Military outfit complete.

Amram and Isechar - dark cloth robes, sand als, ordinary beard and dark wigs.

Hashpo - purple cloth dress, loose fitticg.
Abrath - dark tunic outfit and saedals
Hannh - purple cloth dress loose fitting
Hittipah - red and black combination dress red turban on head.

Girls in white in 2nd act.

3rd act (all dresses long grecian effect)
Adah - sky blue dress, blue scarf around shoulders.

Esther - white dress; Ruth - yellow dress
Electa - bright red; Martha - green dress;
Elizabeth - pink dress; Sarah - yellow dress purple bands around it; Deborah - dark red dress.

DRAMATIS PERSONNEL

JEPTHAH'S DAUGHTER

Jepthah .... A Warriar and Judge of Israel
Amram and Isechar ....Jepthah's Brothers
Hashpo ....Amram's Servant
Abrath ....Jepthah's Servant
Joika and Kishman ....Elders of Israel
Adah ....Jepthah's Daughter
Jewish heroines, friends to Adah:

Ruth	Elizabeth
Esther	Sarah
Martha	Deborah
Electa	

Hannah ....Old Woman, Servant of Jepthah
Hittiphah .... Adah's Maid
Soldiers, band, angels and singers.

Act I.
Scene 1

Room in Gilead's House

Amram and Isechar seated in conversation.

Amram rises and calls Hashpo,—Hashpo, Hashpo, I would speak with thee.

Enter Hashpo, bowing.

Hashpo—Yes, my lord.

Amram—Knowest thou Jepthah, my Father's son?

Hashpo—Yes, my lord?

Amram—Knowest thou his where abouts?

Hashpo—He is with the toilers in the field, my lord.

Amram—Go thou and send him hither. Say thou to him in this wise, "Amram and Isechar, thy father's sons, wants to speak with thee. Make haste and go to them."

Hashpo—I obey thy will, Master.

Exit

[176]

Enter—Jepthah, bowing

Jepthah—My brothers, Hashpo thy servant, bade me come before thee.

Isechar—By what right calleth thou us brothers?

Jepthah—Is not thy father my father? Am I not thy brother?

Isechar—But who is thy mother?

Jepthah—Tell me thy wish and let me be on my way.

Isechar—That is what we want, that you be on your way. Thinkest thou to stay here and inherit our father's house? Get thee out, thou art not a legal child and we, the sons of our father's wife, will inherit our father's house.

Jepthah—If I am not wanted here, then I will go, but remember that the children of Ammon are fierce and war like, and when thou art in trouble, fight thy own battles.

Amram and Isechar—We can fight our own battles without thee. Get thee out. Thou son of a strange woman.

Jepthah—Thy will be done. Fare thee well.
Exit

Amram—Thinkest thou Isechar, that we have acted wisely in driving Jepthah away? He is a mighty man of war and there will come a time when the Ammonites will rise up and drive us out of the land unless we have a leader.

Isechar—Wouldst thou make him leader of our father's house? Wouldst thou make him the ruler of our people? Then if not, let him go his way.

Loud talking outside

Amram—Hark! What noise is that? It is the Ammonites.

Curtain

Act I.

(Scene 2)

Large Room in Jepthah's House—Oriental Furnishings

To be the son of Gilead has meant humiliation and sorrow to me. Here I am, Jepthah, a mighty man of valor, an outcast, driven from my home, to live among strangers here in the land of Job.

I am guilty of no crime, I am not responsible for my parentage, but my brothers drove me out saying, "Get thee out, thou shall not inherit in our father's house, for thou art the son of a strange woman."

Enter two elders of Gilead

Joika—Jepthah, Jepthah, the Ammonites are making war against us—come and be our captain.

Jepthah—Did ye not hate me and drive me out from my father's house? Why are ye come unto me now in thy distress. Get my brother who is the son of my father's wife, to be thy captain.

Kishman—Speak not of these things now Jepthah, thy father's house will be overthrown and thy kinsmen will be slaves to the Ammonites. Come thou and be our leaders and be our head over all of the inhabitants of Gilead.

Jepthah—If ye bring me back to my father's house, and I fight against the children of Ammon, and the Lord deliver them before me, then shall I be your head?

Joika and Kishman (both rise and with uplifted right hands—The Lord be witness between us if we deceive thee, may our bodies be struck with leprosy and may our tongues cleave to the roof of our mouths.

Jepthah—Then it is well, go thy way, I will follow thee when the sun sinketh behind the western hills.

Joika ad Kishman—Tarry not long, the Ammonites are fierce and warlike, and are liable to fall upon us at any moment. Seal this contract with thy shoe.

Jepthah exchanges or gives his right foot shoe to Joika.

Elders exit
(In attitude of prayer)

Jepthah—Lord, God of Israel, if thou wilt without fail deliver the children of Ammon into mine hands, then it shall be that whatsoever cometh forth of the doors of my house to meet me, when I return in peace from the children of Ammon, shall surely be the Lord's and I will offer it up as a burnt offering.

(Rises and calls)

Abrath! Abrath! I would speak with thee.

Enter Abrath—Yes my lord

Jepthah—Go and tell Adah my daughter, that I am returning to my father's country, the land of Gilead, to make war upon the Ammonites, and when the Lord has delivered the children of Ammon into mine hands then will I bring her and my household back into the land of Gilead.

Abrath—Bowing low—Thy orders I'll obey my lord. Exit.

Walks slowly up and down

Jepthah—Alone in meditation, soft music.

Curtain

"What a Friend we have in Jesus," from

concealed orchestra.

Act II.
(Scene 1)

Scene Same as Act I., Scene 2

Adah and group of girls sitting and lounging carelessly about in room. Hannah spinning.

Adah—Girls, my father's slave, Abrath, brought me this message today, that Jepthah, my father, has returned to Gilead to defend the land against the Ammonites, and when the Lord our God shall deliver the Ammonites into his hands, then will he be the acknowledged head of the

House of Gilead, and he shall be the leader of all the people of Gilead, and we will go back into the land and live in peace and happiness.

Girls—joyfully. How lovely! How lovely!

Ruth—But the children of Ammon are a fierce warlike people and if Jepthah fails to conquer them, he'll be slain.

Esther—It hath been said by those of old, that they who put their trust in God will not perish.

Adah—And truly our trust is in the Lord God of hosts.

Sarah—I hope that Jepthah will prove to be a match for the children of Ammon, but I am fearful because they are very fierce.

Deborah—The Ammonites are fierce and warlike, but Jepthah is a mighty warrior and I know that his trust is in the Lord of Hosts and he can not fail.

Elizabeth—Jepthah knows no fear and it is his heart's desire to return to his father's house in the land of Gilead.

Martha—I believe that we shall go back into the land.

Electa—I will surely be one happy soul, because I have grown tired of the people of the land of Job. They are in a way as bad as the Ammonites. They are treacherous and above all dishonest.

(Hannah, still spinning)

Hannah—Speak not so Electa, who can read God's plans? His judgment is past finding out. He hung the stars in the firmament for a purpose. He made the sun to shine and give light to the earth by day, and He made the moon to shine by night. He allowed us to be driven into this strange land for a purpose. And who can tell, but that Jepthah's term of exile in this country is a stepping stone to future greatness?

Girls—Let us hope so at any rate.

(Goes over and puts arm around Adah)

Esther—And for Sweet Adah's sake we hope that Jepthah will be victorious.

Martha—And for our own sake, are we not all of the House of Jepthah?

Elizabeth—Every one of us are of the tribe of Gilead.

Ruth—But I do not remember the land of Gilead, do you Adah?

Adah—No, I too, was young when my father came into this land, but Hannah knows, she was a woman when we came into this land.

Sarah—Hannah is old enough to know everything.

Electa—Hannah tell us something of our homeland, is it beautiful? Is it far away? Are there many good-looking men there?

(Girls gather about Hannah)

Deborah—Yes Hannah, tell us we pray thee, all about our fatherland.

Hannah—Adjusts glasses and with a far away look— Our home is far away, the most beautiful country imaginable. The fertile plains, the rippling brooks, the singing birds, the vineclad hills, the lowing herds, the quiet, peaceful people, are far beyond comparison.

Hittiphah enters unobserved—Loud music outside.

Hittiphah—Adah! Adah! hear the music, thy father hath conquered the Ammonites and the people are rejoicing. All clap hands three times.

Adah—Who brought the glad tidings?

Hittiphah—Abrath thy father's servant hath returned and he says that, like a reaper with a sickle thy father cut down the Ammonites, and he bid thee to make ready to return to the land of Gilead.

Adah—Where is my father? Where is my father?

(Music continues louder and louder)

"Onward Christian Soldiers" concealed choir.

Enter Abrath.

Abrath—Where is Adah? Where is Adah?

Adah—what tiding Abrath?

Abrath—Thy father is the mightiest warrior in all the world, he hath conquered the children of Ammon.

Adah—God's name be praised.
All gather joyfully around Adah, and stand in semi-circle with uplifted eyes and hands.

Curtain

Scene II. of Act II.
(Scene Highway)

Enter band playing "Onward Christian Soldiers," and Jepthah followed by soldiers and group of people from right.
Enter Adah followed by group of girls—from left girls with tambourines, flutes and various stringed musical instruments making merry.
Adah—Hail my father, mightiest man of Israel! Long live Jepthah.
Girls—Long live Jepthah. All hail; all hail; all hail, Jepthah.

Jepthah—In agony wails—Alas my daughter.

Adah—My father state thy woes.

Jepthah—Thou hast brought me very low and thou art one of them that trouble me.

Adah—Why accuse me thus? What have I done?

Jepthah—I have made a vow unto the Lord and I can not go back.

Adah—What was thy vow?

Jepthah—I vowed unto the Lord, that if he would deliver the Ammonites into my hands, that I would offer as burnt offering the first that came out of the door of my house to meet me, and lo it is thee. My only child.

(Embraces Adah and sobs aloud)

Adah—My father if thou hast made this vow unto the Lord, do to me that which hath proceeded out of thy mouth.

Jepthah—My child! My child! My only child!

(Releases Adah and sinks to floor)

Adah—Let me go to the mountains and prepare to meet my God, at the end of two months I'll return ready to be offered up.

Ruth—Adah as the Lord liveth I will accompany thee to the mountains.

Esther—And I will also go with thee and try to comfort thee.

Martha—On the mountain top with the blue sky for our shelter and the green grass for our carpet and the pale moon for our light by night, I'll abide with thee.

Electa—No woman has died to save her father's honor, and since thou wilt be the first, I'll stay with thee to the end. Because we love one another.

Adah leads the way, they walk slowly around stage three times singing, "If Jesus Goes with Me I'll Go." Girls exit at left, other group watch sadly as they go out.

Curtain

Act III.

(Scene 1)

A Woodland Scene—Altar Built of Sticks Laid Crosswise, a Little Back of Center of Stage—Light Shining Up Through Sticks

All members of play standing in group at left of stage. Jepthah, standing near altar, sword in hand—soft music.

Enter—Adah, Ruth, Esther, Martha and Electa, forming a perfect star.

Adah—Jepthah my father, I am come to be offered up

[183]

in fulfillment of thy vow.

Jepthah—Lord God of Israel, give me the needed strength to perform my vow unto thee—steps over to Adah and covers her face—Adah removes veil.

Ruth—Adah uncover thy face, thou hast committed no crime.

Jepthah—I can not slay my child looking in her face.

Esther—She is as pure as the morning dew, and only a criminal's face is hidden during execution.

Martha—Since it is the will of God, Jepthah, perform thy task, I believe in the ressurection—we will see Adah again.

Adah moves nearer Jepthah—My father here I am.

Electa—Let us love one another, as Adah hath shown love for her father and the peace that passeth all understanding will flood our souls.
Adah standing with veil held in both hands across head.

Group sings, "Sweet Peace is Flooding my Soul."
I feel in my heart a blessing divine,
 'Tis sweet as the music of heaven—
It fills all my soul with wonderful peace
 Since Jesus my sins has forgiven.

CHORUS
Peace, peace, wonderful peace,
 Since Jesus my all doth control
Peace, peace, wonderful peace;
 Sweet peace is flooding my soul.

O wonderful peace, O spirit of rest,
 A calm that allays all my fears,
'Tis filling my heart with love that shall last
 Thru all of eternity's years.

Today I shall rise to mansions on high,
 Beholding my Lord on his throne;
And singing anew of wonderful peace,
 There dwelling as one of his own.

Jepthah standing near Adah with drawn sword, pulls the veil over her face, she carries it back as before, leaning as far back as possible, holding veil in both hands across back of head.

Girls form semi-circle around alter and clasp hands over head and look upward.

> O look yonder what I see
> Coming to carry me home.
> A band of angels coming after me
> Coming to carry me home.
>
> O just see what I behold
> Coming to carry me home.
> Angels from the throne of gold
> Coming to carry me home.

Angel band appear in background

Men stand with bowed heads, arms folded.

Jepthah kills Adah with sword at close of "Swing Low." Song. Abrath and Amram catches Adah as she falls and places body on burning altar.

Curtain

PRINCE OF PEACE

CHARACTERS

Angel of the Lord
Mary
Joseph
Infant Jesus
Shepherds (6)
Three Wise Men
Neighbors
Angel Band
King Herod

Courtiers and Slaves of King (2)
Queen Herodias
Attendants (2)
Warning Angel
Simeon
Anna (Phrophetess)

All Costumes Oriental

Act I.
In Joseph's House

Angel of the Lord Appears to Joseph
Joseph (asleep on couch)

Angel—Joseph! Joseph! Oh Joseph! Thou son of David, fear not to take unto thee Mary, thy wife, for that which is conceived in her is of the Holy Ghost.

(Joseph Drowses)

Joseph—Who art thou? and from whence comest thou?

Angel—I am the angel of the Lord and have come to tell you that Mary, your wife, shall bring forth a son and thou shalt call his name Jesus.

Joseph—What shall be the mission of this child?

Angel—He shall save his people from their sins. Do you not remember Isaih's prophecy? "For unto us a Child is born, unto us a Son is given, and the government shall be upon his shoulders. His name shall be called Wonderful, Councellor, the Mighty God, the Everlasting Father, the Prince of Peace."

Go thou and tell Mary the glad news. Rejoice and be exceeding glad, it is the work of God.

Angel   Exit

Joseph sits in meditation.
Enter Mary

Mary—Joseph, did I not hear you talking with someone?

Joseph—Yes, the Angel of the Lord was here and commanded me saying: "Tell Mary, thy wife, that she shall bring forth a son, and his name shall be Jesus."

Mary—Why did you not call me so that I, myself might have seen the Angel?

Joseph—He did not ask for thee, he gave me the message. Fear not!

Mary—I can hardly realize that I, a poor Jewish maiden am to become the mother of the promised Messiah.

Enter Neighbors—they speak

Joseph, Mary, What tidings have you? The Angel of the Lord was seen leaving thy house.

Joseph—The Angel told me that Mary shall bring forth a Son, who shall take away the sins of all the people and the government shall rest upon his shoulder and his name shall be the Mighty God, the Everlasting Father, the Prince of Peace.

Mary—Yes, and we are to call him Jesus.

Neighbors—How wonderful! Such beautiful words. Such wonderful words.
Oh! How wonderful to know that the Prince of Peace is near.

Oh Wonderful Words

"Sing them over again to me,
Wonderful words of life.
Let me more of their beauty see
Wonderful words of life
Words of life and beauty

[189]

Teach me faith and duty,
Beautiful words, wonderful words,
Wonderful words of life.
Beautiful words, wonderful words,
Wonderful words of life.
Wonderful words of life.
Sinners, hearken this wond'rous call
Wonderful words of life.
Christ is coming to die for all,
All so freely given, wooing us to heaven
Beautiful words, wonderful words,
Wonderful words of life.
Beautiful words, wonderful words,
Wonderful words of life."

Act II.
(Scene 1.)

Palace of the King

Herod on Throne
Queen on Throne
Attendants stand around
(Some with faces on floor)
(Some kneeling, some fanning queen)
Enter Wise Men

Melchar—O King, live forever. We received thy message and have come at thy command.

King—It is rumored that there is a child somewhere in my realm who was born to be King of the Jews, and I understand that you are on your way to see and worship the young child. Go and find him and bring me a true report so that I may go also and worship him.

Gaspar—O King, we are strangers in this land and might not be able to find our way back to you.

King—A crazy man can find the palace of the King and it will not fard well with thee if thou failest to come back to me with information concerning this child.

Third Wise Man—We heed thy words, O King, let

us depart in peace.

Queen—Ere you depart, hear my words. Upon your return, I will banquet you in the royal palace. My servants shall serve you, you shall be the guests of the King and Queen. Only bring us correct information, because I too, want to carry gifts to the young child and worship at his shrine.

Wise Men—We will ponder in our hearts all of thy words.

Exit Wise Men

King—As soon as these men return I shall make ready and go down and slay the child. He must not live to overthrow my kingdom.

Queen—Take me with thee, O King, that I might see the child who was born to be King of the Jews. A great pity it will be to slay this innocent child.

King—Knowest thou not that it has been said that old things shall pass away at the coming of this child, that means that our kingdom shall be overthrown, and you and I will no longer occupy this throne.

Queen—Your words make me faint. How could I live away from the throne? Hark! I hear bugles calling. Come, investigate the cause.

Curtain

Act II.
(Scene 2)

Shepherds on Judeas Plain

Three Wise Men

Shepherds seated on ground conversing with each other

Angel of the Lord appears

Angel—Fear not. I am come to bring thee good tidings of great joy. For unto you is born today in the town of Bethlehem, a Savior who is Christ, the Son of God. Peace on Earth, Good Will to All Men.

[191]

Angel band appear singing.
"Joy to the world, the Lord is come,
Let earth receive her King.
Let every heart prepare him room
Let heaven and nature sing
Let heaven and nature sing
Let heaven and nature sing"

Angels Exit

Enter Wise Men

Wise Men—How far is Bethlehem away?

Shepherds—Across the hill on yonder plain. Are you looking for the new born King?

Wise Men—We have journeyed from the east. We have traveled fast and far. We are searching for the Prince of Peace. We are guided by a beautiful star.

Shepherds—We know that he is born. A band of Angels came and told us the good news.

We too, are going to see the babe of Bethlehem. We will follow thee.

Act III.

Mary
Babe in Manger
Wise men come and worship infant
Shepherds and children with gifts worship infant
Joseph standing by
Angel band singing

Pantomime and Song

Silent night, holy night,
All is calm, all is bright,
Round yon virgin mother and child,
Holy infant, so tender and mild.
Sleep in heavenly peace,
Sleep in heavenly peace,
Silent night, holy night,
Shepherds kneel at the sight,
Glories stream from afar.
Angels sing the hallelelujah,
Comes the glorious morn
Comes the glorious morn

Silent night, holy night,
Shineth now, God's pure light,
Radiant beams from thy holy face,
Bring the dawn of redeeming grace,
Peace and heavenly love,
Peace and heavenly love.

While song is being sung, Wise Men enter and kneel, bestowing gifts, then Shepherds, the children, then neighbors, all kneel in circle around Manger.

Angels continue singing.

Curtain

BACHELORS' CONVENTION

A Comedy Drama in Three Acts

For Twelve Young Men and Twenty-four
Young Women.

CHARACTERS

Professor Ernest Knowall........................Pres. of Convention
Harry Listen ....Sec'y of Convention
David Woman Hater........................Treas. of Convention
James Disgusted
John Workhard
Jack Simple
Richard Sleepyhead
Fred Clumsy
Doctor Hurry
Rev. Solomon Makepeace
Frank Forgetful
Tom Hardluck
Jane Stout..Supt. of Nurses Assn.
Frances Lean...Asst. Supt. Assn.
Mary Short ....Sec'y Nurses' Assn.
Emma Long ....Treas. Nurses' Assn.

COSTUMES

Knowall—attired as an old school-master, wears three
   pairs of eye-glasses.
Listen—wears two pairs of eye-glasses.
Workhard—overalls and jumper.
Simple—dunce cap, and red trousers and green semi-
   fitting coat.
Sleepyhead—sloven fitting old suit.
Doctor Hurry—English walking suit and beard Van-
   dyke.
Rev. Makepeace—Ministers garb.
Others—ordinary dress.
Girls—attired as nurses, white one-piece dress and
   nurses' cap.

First Act

Men sitting and some standing around in room, casually talking aloud with each other. There are two tables, the president is to sit at one, the secretary at the other.

Enter president from a side door—takes his place and sounds a gavel.

President—Gentlemen, come to order and be seated.

All find seats

President—Secretary please call roll of officers and members.

Secretary calls names, each answers as his name is called, (saving sleepyhead).

Sleepyhead who sits on a front seat asleep, wakes up just as the roll is finished and jumps to his feet exclaiming, "You didn't call my name. You didn't call my name, I am a member here.

President—Yes, Sleepyhead your name was called, but you sleep so much you won't hear Gabriel blow.

Sleepyhead—Well, I hear you blowing and you ain't Gabriel.

President—Sounds gavel and angrily says: "Will you sit down, Mr. Sleepyhead?"

President—Secretary, read the minutes of the last meeting.

Secretary adjusts glasses and reads:

City of Hollygog, State of Nowhere

February 41st, 19,099.

Bachelors' Convention met at their headquarters at 13.85 p. m. All officers and members present.

After the meeting was duly opened by the president, the business of the convention was dispatched in due form. There was no new business. The convention adjourned to meet again at the call of the president.

Professor Ernest Knowall, president; Honorable Mr. Harry Listen, secretary.

President—Gentlemen you have heard the reading of the minutes of the last meeting; what is your pleasure?

Hardluck—I move you Mr. President that the minutes stand approved as read.

Forgetful—I second the motion.

President—It has been moved by Mr. Hardluck and seconded by Mr. Forgetful that the minutes stand approved as read.

Forgetful—No sir, I didn't second any motion, what motion?

President—Mr. Forgetful if your memory is so short as that please don't second any more motions here.

Forgetful—I didn't second any motion.

Men—Question! Question!

President—As many as favor the motion, let it be known by standing.

All stand but Womanhater, Sleepyhead and Workhard.

President—Mr. Womanhater, Mr. Sleepyhead and Mr. Workhard, what are your objections.

Womanhater—I was busy counting money and that slipped by me, (still counting small money.)

Beg your pardon.

Workhard—Mr. President, after a man works hard all day and comes home and cooks his own supper and patches the holes in his own breeches, he certainly doesn't feel like making himself a bouncing ball.

Sleepyhead—I was taking a little nap and didn't quite understand what was going on (yawns) but what ever it is its alright.

Disgusted—Really Sleepyhead you are a nuisance,

you and Forgetful remind me of a henpecked husband, whose quarrelling wife and screaming brats make him forget all that he ever knew.

Simple—I'll say they do.

President—Alright, (sounds gavel) is the committee on resolutions ready to report. Secretary please name the committee.

Secretary reads their names and they come forward.

Rev. Solomon Makepeace.

Mr. Frederick Clumsy (Clumsy stumbles) over someone's feet and falls while coming to his place and says: "Move your feet, Doctor Hurry."

Simple—I am on that committee.

Secretary—I think not Mr. Simple.

President—Simple, you are out of order.

Simple—I am always out of order when I speaks up for my honors.

(Simple joins committee)

President sounds gavel, says, "Read."

Makepeace adjusts glasses and reads—Mr. President, officers and members of Bachelors' Convention, we, your committee on resoultions, beg to submit the following:

Dr. Hurry will read the resolutions.

Hurry reads:

Where as we are a band of single gentlemen, living in quietude and happiness in this our building on the sea shore, washing for ourselves, cooking for ourselves, mending and sewing for ourselves and thinking for ourselves and breathing for ourselves, be it resolved that this place remain free from disturbance and unrest. Be it further resolved that no woman, frill, flounce, petticoat, basque or bonnet ever be allowed to cross the threshold of this door.

All—good! Good! That's fine.

(All clap their hands)

Be it further resolved that no member of this convention ever speak to a woman again during his natural life.

(Prolonged applause)

Signed

Frederick Clumsy, Doctor Hurry and Rev. Solomon Makepeace.

Committee

Simple—Why didn't you read my name. I'm on this committee, Jack Simple.

President—This seems to meet the approval of all.

All—Yes! Yes! Yes! !

Hardluck—What is the hour of the night?

Clumsy—Bedtime I'm sure, because my feet are getting heavy.

(All laugh hilariously)

Workhard—Since I must get up early I'll say goodnight.

President—Gentlemen we are ready to close.

All sing

A band of bachelors are we
We are from care and women free,
No crying babes or quarreling wives
To interfere our happy lives.

Curtain

Act II.

(Disordered Room)

Simple—washing clothes.

Hardluck—ironiing shirt.

Sleepyhead—stretched out on couch asleep.

President and Secretary—reading.

Makepeace—patching his trousers.

Hurry—sewing buttons on pants.

Forgetful—on knees scrubbing floor.

Womanhater—seated at table writing.

Disgusted—seated looking at quite a number of women's pictures then tearing them to shreds throwing them on floor.

Enter Workhard with cabbage in hand and Clumsy with sack of potatoes, he drops them and they roll all over floor.

Harduck—Well my name is Hardluck and I really am having hardluck, I've burned my shirt tail off.

Workhard—puts cabbage on table and drops into chair. "Boys I am really tired."

Ladies enter timidly

Men look horrified and wave them to go back—women advance and men huddle in a corner as though frightened at the sight of them.

All the girls say: "Miss Stout, you speak."

Miss Stout—Gentlemen, we are fully aware that this is Bachelors' Headquarters, but we are a band of nurses whose mission is to administer to the sick, heal the wounded, care for the afflicted and help the distressed and—

Simple—Nobody here sick, nobody here wounded, nobody here afflicted or distressed.

President—Hear what they have to say.

Miss Lean—O! sirs, our ship was wrecked across the bar, there were one hundred of us and only twenty-four survived.

Womanhater—Twenty-four too many survived.

[200]

Miss Lean—This was the only house that we saw. We did not ignore the sign that we saw across the door, "Bachelors' Headquarters." But we knew that if you were men, you had hearts, and that at sometime in your lives you have had homes and mothers' love, therefore we ventured to cross your door sill and beg for shelter from the storm tonight.

President—What is your name?

Miss Lean—My name is Frances Lean.

President—It ought to be Frances Lawyer.

President—Gentlemen, you have heard the plea of these er-er-ahem! these ship-wrecked folks. What is your pleasure?

Dr. Hurry—We have no pleasure or room either.

Miss Long sweeps past the crowd and dramatically falls on her knees at Dr. Hurry's feet, and exclaims: "For the sake of your sainted mother, whose portrait you carry near your heart, have mercy on us and take us in."

Dr. Hurry staggers backward and sobs aloud, "Oh, holy smokes! it's the ghost of my missionary sister who died in China. Let them stay! Let them stay!!

Rev. Makepeace—I move you, Mr. President, that we let them stay tonight.

Listen—I second the motion.

Simple and Clumsy—But where are we going to stay if they stay here?

President—Gentlemen, you two are out of order. There is a motion before us.

Simple—Yes, you'll be out of order when you have no place to sleep.

President (sounds gavel)—Shut up, Simple!

President—It has been moved and duly seconded that we allow these er-er-er women (gulps) er folks to stay here tonight. Are you ready for the question?

"Not ready, not ready," from every one but Make-peace, Listen and Dr. Hurry.

President—Gentlemen, state your unreadiness.

Men—Unreadiness, why, where are we going to sleep tonight?

Miss Short—Gentlemen, we ask not for the privilege of sleeping. Allow us to sit here in your assembly hall. Lie down and take your rest.

Disgusted—Well, I am only one man, but I want to ask, have you all forgotten our resolutions? Let them stay here tonight and mark my word, they'll steal from you.

Miss Short—We are nurses, not thieves.

Disgusted—Every woman is a terrible thief; she will steal your heart, and what's greater than a man's heart? But suit yourselves, boys.

Miss Long—Only trust us, gentlemen; the storm is raging on the outside and there is not another house on the island. Won't you let us stay? We will not steal your house, we will not steal your hats, neither will we steal your hearts. Only let us stay, sheltered from the storm.

Listen—There's a motion before the house.

President—Is there further objections? Three times (sounds gavel), motion is carried.

Sleepyhead (wakes up)—What's that? What's that? Who are these? What are these? Where did they come from? What do they want?

Forgetful—I think they are women, and they were sent here to nurse us.

President—Day breaks at 15 o'clock and you folks can leave then. Boys, we'll retire. (Pantomime.) Men all shy away, some crawl out, some back out, some run out, as though afraid. Girls sit in chairs and begin to nod; some lean over on table. Lights grow dimmer and dimmer until they finally go out.

Curtain

Act III.

Same room as in Act 2, but in perfect order; a large table in rear of room with snow-white linen cloth, all set up for the dinner meal; vase of flowers in center of table—real dinner on table, in covered dishes

Men enter, some from right and some from left. They look about bewildered and astonished; they peer into corners and all around and whisper among themselves. Clumsy dares to lift the lid of one of the dishes and drops lid and exclaims, "Oh, boys, look here!" Men open dishes and look surprised.

Disgusted—Can this be real?

Womanhater—I wonder if those were real women or were they angels; and where have they gone? All sit and begin to eat.

Simple—I don't care what they are; I want one of them.

President—Well, this reminds one of home. Fellows, has it ever occurred to you what a dear place home was? Some of our homes were humble, but be it ever so humble, there is no place like home.

Singing in the distance—Home, Sweet Home.

Men listen while they eat.

Singing grows softer and further away.

Forgetful—I think, like Womanhater, that those were angels. Do you hear them singing? Why, those are heavenly voices.

Dr. Hurry—Oh, if we had only been more courteous to them, but now they are gone forever.

Makepeace—We must use more common sense in the future.

Simple—I am going to use some common sense now. I am going to get me a wife.

Hardluck—I wish that we could find a hot dinner and a clean home to come into every night.

Listen—And so do I.

Workhard—You all can suit yourselves, but I am going to—going to-er-er get me a-a-wife, because I am a hard working man and I want to rest when I come home.
Sleepyhead—Are you folks letting a meal of victuals turn your heads?

Men—Not a meal of victuals, Sleepyhead, but a change in our conditions.

Sleepyhead—A change in your conditions? Why, how are you going to change them? You can't marry each other, and those women are gone.

Ladies have entered from the rear, unobserved.
All Ladies—Gentemen, we were gone, but we've ventured back to thank you for your kindness to us.

Simple—Angels, er-ladies-er-women, girls or whatever you are, we've decided to get us some wives. Won't you marry us?

President—Simple, you are always out of order.

Simple—We are all out of order, then.

President—Ladies, won't you spend the evening and as long as you wish?
Ladies—We thank you, kind sir, but knowing that this is a bachelors' headquarters, we will not impose upon you by staying longer. God be with you till we meet again.

Sing "God Be With You Till We Meet Again."
Simple—But we are not going to part; you will either stay with us or we will go with you.

Ladies—We dare not stay here, and you cannot go with us.

Fare Thee Well

Men rush forward and on bended knees, say "We pray thee stay. We have a message for thee."

Ladies look bewildered, and try to back away. Men advance on knees.

President—Ladies, we can no longer live without you.

Ladies, with uplifted hands—What do you mean? What do you mean?

President—We mean that this is no longer Bachelors' Headquarters, since you've graced it with your presence. It will be heaven on earth if you will but only er (gulps) marry us.

Ladies look at each other in astonishment.

If we should come here to live, where would you sleep? You haven't room for us.

Men—We'll sleep on the floor, or out of doors, or any place. We'll work for you, we'll live for you, we'll die for you, we'll steal for you, we'll go to jail for you, and we've a preacher here in our midst who can perform the ceremony.

Miss Stout—You have spoken well, but there are 24 of us and only 12 of you.

Rev. Makepeace—Have you forgotten that Solomon had more than one wife? Me myself, I can support five.

Sleepy and Clumsy—Any of can support five or more.

Miss Stout—Let me talk it over with my ladies. Ladies go into deep private conversation.

Miss Stout (says slowly)—Gentlemen, we have er-er-agreed to marry you.

Men—Good! Good!

Miss Stout—But you will have to agree to the following (coughs): Stay home at night, and take care of the babies, while WE attend our club meetings; bring home your money untouched and give us every penny; and when we have company, stay out in the kitchen, or down in the cellar, and at all times be subservient to our will. (Long pause.) Do you agree?

Men all nod their heads.

Miss Stout—I do not understand signs; your answer must be yes or no.

Men (reluctantly)—Yes.

Simple (aside)—Promises, like pie crusts, are easily broken.

Dr. Hurry—Well, there is no need of all this quandary. Rev. Makepeace, you are a preacher. Can't you er-er-er marry us to these ladies?

Makepeace—Gladly will I perform the ceremony, but you know that I am going to marry, too, and who's going to perform my ceremony?

Simple—Man, can't you marry yourself as you marry the rest of us?

Makepeace—Yes, gentlemen; select your wives and line up. (Lights dim.) Men approach ladies and talk in undertones.

Each man walks triumphantly up and down the platform with two ladies, with the exception of Knowall, who has four, and Hurry, who has four, and Simple, who is alone. Sleepyhead, who was nodding, wakes and exclaims—What's happened? What is this? What you all doing, getting married, eh? All the ladies gone? Where's mine? This is not a square deal.

Simple—Sleepy, follow me.

They rise and stand, and as the others pass, Simple presses himself between two of the ladies with Knowall, and falls into line.

Rev. Makepeace—Ladies and Gentlement, the time has arrived to put an end to our single wickedness, instead of blessedness, and now by the high power in me vested I declare us all, men and wives.

Men all—So may it be.

(Song "Coming through the Rye" with gestures.)

Curtain
End

ABOUT THE EDITORS

Henry Louis Gates, Jr., is the W. E. B. Du Bois Professor of the Humanities, Chair of the Afro-American Studies Department, and Director of the W. E. B. Du Bois Institute for Afro-American Research at Harvard University. One of the leading scholars of African-American literature and culture, he is the author of *Words, Signs, and the Racial Self* (1987), *The Signifying Monkey: A Theory of Afro-American Literary Criticism* (1988), *Loose Canons: Notes on the Culture Wars* (1992), and the memoir *Colored People* (1994).

Jennifer Burton is in the Ph.D. program in English Language and Literature at Harvard University. She is the volume editor of *The Prize Plays and Other One-Acts* in this series. She is a contributor to *The Oxford Companion to African-American Literature* and to *Great Lives from History: American Women*. With her mother and sister she coauthored two one-act plays, *Rita's Haircut* and *Litany of the Clothes*. Her fiction and personal essays have appeared in *Sun Dog, There and Back*, and *Buffalo*, the Sunday magazine of the *Buffalo News*.

P. Jane Splawn is Adjunct Professor of the Humanities at Indiana University. She is currently at work on a critical analysis of contemporary black women's drama and ritual, and continues to teach and write on nineteenth- and twentieth-century black women's drama, literature, and feminist theory.